DIVER
A PROFESSIONAL DIVER'S STORY

By Tony Smith

VanJus Press
Galveston

Photographs and Original Drawings	Tony Smith
Cover Photographs	Terry Stern (also by Terry Stern: photographs in plates 13, 14, 15, and 16)
Cover Design and Layout	Justine Gilcrease

ISBN 0-9666438-3-6
©Copyright 2000 by VanJus Press,
1618 23rd St., Galveston, TX 77550
All Rights Reserved
(409) 762-2333, FAX (409) 762-0411

CONTENTS

    PREFACE **1**
1 LOADING OUT A JOB **5**
2 ARRIVE JOB SITE **11**
3. PLANNING YOUR DIVE **17**
4. TENDERS **21**
5. WATER ENTRY: LOOK BEFORE YOU LEAP **27**
6. CURRENTS **33**
7. PENETRATION **39**
8. OILFIELD **43**
      JACKET/PLATFORM PLACEMENT **43**
      PIPELINE CONSTRUCTION **48**
      PIPELINE DREDGING AND JET SLEDS **51**
      RISER CONSTRUCTION **55**
      PIGS IN THE PIPE **56**
      RIG DIVING **58**
9. ATTITUDE ADJUSTMENTS **69**
10. DAM DIVING **73**
11. ENVIRONMENTAL DIVING **79**
12. TREASURE, ARCHEOLOGY AND ARTIFACTS **95**
13. COMING UP FREE **105**
14. FREE DIVING **109**
15. FISHISTORIES **119**
16. GOLF BALLS AND THE MIDNIGHT FROGMEN **129**
17. JOB HUNTING DURING THE BLACK GOLD RUSH **139**
19. DIVING SCHOOLS **147**

DEDICATED TO THOSE LOST IN THE WORK

PREFACE

Since my first underwater project of capturing hermit crabs by grabbing them from tide pools near San Francisco as a child, the child grew with technology. A faceplate of plexiglass mounted in a mask of gum rubber could be cleared with a little spit, and froggy green fins could propel me into deeper tide pools and grottos, far from the drone of a 7th grade teacher's discourse of watered-down history. Snorkels arrived on the scene as THE great boon of my diving technology in those days, with SCUBA running a close second, SCUBA having a limited air supply and being cumbersome and useless once the air was gone.

The military imposed SCUBA training on me, and I found myself teaching service personnel in its use, and then being sent to search for the Navy's lost anchors in Buckner Bay, Okinawa. Out of the service, my brother recruited me for dredging in the Yuba river in the Sierra Mountains, ostensibly for gold.

For many of us, the sea beckons with its depth-hidden mysteries, blue lines descending through a mist of plankton into a mother of creation, drawing us to her. This allure is sometimes hard to remember when, hanging for countless moments that seem like years in a dark void on a decompression stop in ..., what ocean is this? We have given ourselves to the work.

We will grit our teeth, clothe ourselves in layers of stiff rubber, and tie ourselves to the midstream anchor that keeps the diver from being washed away by the Yuba River.

This book is about the work, with emphasis given, to safe procedures to accomplish the work and remain healthy.

The variety of underwater work underlines the fact that life support systems, vital to breathing while underwater, are merely the vehicle by which we go to work. Great importance is given to doing the work, but only as it does not conflict with those life support systems. Sometimes it would seem that those in charge over underwater works do not realize that dead divers do not work well, at all. It is your responsibility to set safe procedures for yourself, and not be dissuaded by the aura of urgency that so often attends underwater work projects.

On several occasions I have quit jobs due to safety concerns, and there would be another diver eager to take my place and take the chances that I would not take. This has been a problem with divers and, ultimately with diving contractors, throughout the years that I have worked in the underwater. One such contractor lost eight divers in one year. There is a saying that there are old divers, and bold divers, but there are no old, bold divers.

Some of these chapters are dedicated to friends and colleagues lost in the work.

Some chapters will take a look at the nature of social life ashore in the society of divers, particularly on the Gulf Coast and international oilfield diving communities and so, perhaps glean some clues, as to the nature of the beast.

Underwater work is one of the few occupations, like sports, in which the individual can excel, but only as a part of a team, if the work is in deep water. Over time, you will be rewarded for what you put into team effort, even to the example of quitting a job, only to he replaced by some bold loner.

My interest in history has been gratified by treasure diving, or Marine Archeology, if you will, a realm that is discussed in this book. But I know of no comprehensive history that describes the descent from shallow water into the deep made by oilfield divers, which is a fairly recent event. As pioneers to the dark continents beneath the waves, American divers may one day rate with earlier explorers credited with the discovery of new lands, in another sort of hostile environment.

Divers are now being replaced by robots in many tasks, in the great depths, while development of new, lightweight armored suits and scuba units capable of any depth for 12-hour durations are being perfected, signaling the return of underwater human workers at great depths. Once the barriers of required mixed-gas and decompression are passed, there is no way to foretell what wealth awaits humanity in deep marine explorations.

A new generation of divers will be shuttled to work while never being required to endure the increased pressures now associated with deep underwater work, even when they may choose to venture outside of the habitats that will be established at the bottom of the sea.

1.

LOADING OUT A JOB
Dedicated to Gene Heme, Morgan City

The routine for loading out a diving job requires a lot of attention to detail. Most diving companies will require you, as a member of the designated dive team, to go over the equipment to be used on a given job preparatory to its being loaded out the door onto trucks for transport to some distant port or helicopter pad for the ride offshore.

Any machinery such as compressor or water pump or welding machine should be test-run to your satisfaction, and state of wear on hoses and fittings, communication wires and radio should be considered and replaced, where necessary.

figure 1-Typical workboat, Gulf of Mexico, 100-200 ft. long.

Perhaps you are on call, and in the middle of some festive event or French Quarter bar your pager goes off. You call in to learn that you are going to be required to pick up some gear at Bonjour Diving Company, then drive 400 miles to a swamp, where you will go underwater to repair a leak in an oil pipeline, for Muskrat Oil Transport Company. It is now one in the morning, and you wish you had not had those last couple of drinks, but you tell them okay, you'll be there soon, hang up, then you dial your tender's phone number. You coordinate a meeting with the tender, either to have them (or someone) come get you, or take a cab to meet them at the shop. They will drive the distance to the job, estimating 8 hours travel time, while you get some rest and sober up. Since you will be working in shallow water, you may well have to spend an

PERHAPS YOU ARE ON CALL, AND IN THE MIDDLE OF SOME FESTIVE EVENT, YOUR PAGER GOES OFF

figure 2- Dawn departure for Main Pass, Gulf of Mexico.

figure 3-Anchored in the river near the Gulf of Mexico, two workboats stand by for the passing of a hurricane that is in the Gulf. Note dive hose, chambers.

extended period underwater at maximum labor capacity. You'd better be able to do it, or decline the job.

I once had a contractor's dispatcher call me and tell me that they would send the tender they had selected in their company truck, in which all the gear I would need was already loaded, to pick me up at home and convey me to the dock where we were scheduled to go offshore. Great, thought I, what luxurious service! All I had to do was grab my helmet and personal gear, go offshore and make a gravy dive to put a simple cap on a wellhead at 100 foot depth. Easy money, right?

But as we are unloading the gear onto the crew boat preparatory to going offshore and I am looking it over, everything looks okay, except the hose. It looks too short. It turns out that I've got an eighty-foot hose to make a hundred foot dive. The 'hurry hurry' element has struck again.

When you may be required to drive great distances to destinations you are not familiar with, draw a map, and stop to call the dispatcher at any time you suspect that you may be off track.

Nobody can accurately predict what oceans and weather may do unexpectedly offshore, so when you put that gear aboard the crew boat, be sure to dog things down as tight as possible.

Close the hatches on the decompression chambers while transporting them. I know of one instance where a chamber was washed overboard in a squall (a small, but sometimes furious, localized storm) such as often occur on the Gulf of Mexico in summer. Because the hatches had been dogged, the chamber was later found, floating in a calm sea.

Weather reports cannot be counted on. One barge Captain that I worked for frequently would often shut the work down when the weather report indicated rough weather, even though in actuality the sea was calm, and not a cloud in the sky. The Captain would convene a booray card game in the day room of the barge, a sort of cutthroat card game of Cajun extraction, and the game would progress until either the Captain had won everyone's money, or he got a good weather report, then we'd go back to work. Advice: You cannot win a booray game with the Captain, and are better off to enjoy the good weather.

Air Travel: So you're on your way. You have your copy of a fat 18-month contract with Monolith Divers, Inc. in your pocket, have put your helmet in the overhead compartment, adjusted your seatbelt, and are grinning at your own reflection as you look out the window of the 747 PanAm flight for Rio as it taxies toward the runway.

Don't ever ship your headgear with your luggage, or you may never see it again. And don't show off by putting it on while you're on the plane. If anyone's curious, tell them it's an antique TV set. Get some rest. You don't know what may be in store for you during the trip by way of long lines through customs and ticket counters. You may have to make a deep dive with your jetlag many hours from now, and only moments after you get to the job site. They probably need you there, or you wouldn't be going.

If you are merely flying offshore from Morgan City to a drilling rig in the Gulf of Mexico, you might say a prayer. One chapter is dedicated to Gene Heme, whose 'copter went down in the swamp. And remember, don't get airborne in any type of aircraft for at least 18 hours after a decompression dive. Ride crew boats, when you can, so as to avoid working-day thrills that you don't get paid for.

On being inebriated, drunk, stoned, tore up (or down), wasted, tripping, stumbling, or obviously insane, please don't show up at the job in any such condition. You'll be fired, run off, blackballed, maybe even busted. Dope-sniffing dogs will bite you, and twelve righteous jurors indict you, and you might fall overboard while attempting to walk on water. Anyway, that has already been done. Save it, please for after work, if for no other reason, it could cost you and your company a lot of $$$$$$.

Plate 1-The ones that talk to their helmets have been offshore for 18 months.

Plate 2-Currents can take you away.

Plate 3-Threading the needle.

Plate 4-Scooter Rescue on the stinger.

2.

ARRIVE JOB SITE
Dedicated to Terry Griggs, Gretna

You have arrived at the job site, be it a rusted barge on a blackwater canal, or a drill ship on the deep blue of the South Atlantic, you note the time and date in your personal log. You maintain this log, ongoing. Have the Supervisor put his signature on it for each day.

You are a long ways from your last eel meal.

But before you eat, stow your gear out of the way, out of the weather, and where it won't invite theft.

figure 4- Double-lock decompression chambers such as pictured here are typical of all but the most shallow water jobs of 40 ft. or less depth.

Your gear stored, look up the Diving Supervisor to learn where you will bunk, and when you may expect to make a dive. If you are to dive soon, you should eat sparingly. Once you have located your bunk, consider what possible escape routes you might take from its location, in case of fire or some other emergency. Then, go on deck.

Seek out the Dive Station, and find out if there is a dive planned, or in progress, and take a look at the diving decompression schedule that is being used. Make your own inspection of the life support systems, mixed gas and air supply, compressor back-up capabilities, PT or bell systems, and the rigging of these items. Ask the tenders if they are aware of any problems with anything. The lead tender should know.

IF YOU ARE TO DIVE SOON, YOU SHOULD EAT SPARINGLY.

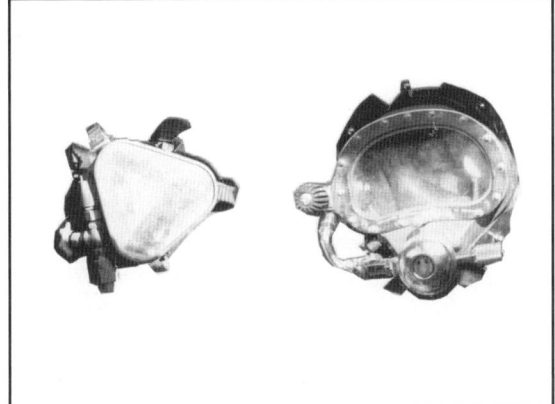

figure 5 - Desco free-flow mask (left) and Kirby demand regulator mask (right).

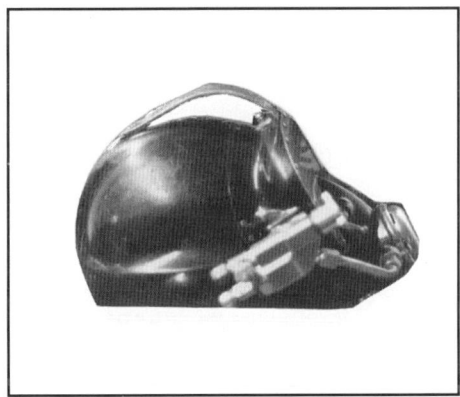

figure 6 - Aquadyne DM-7 diving helmet.

Use only your own head gear if that is possible. Sometimes that is not possible, say, in the case of mixed gas diving, if and when the diving company you are employed by requires you to use their headgear. That will probably mean that they are using one of the recirculator or closed circuit breathing apparatus to save on mixed gas expenditures. If you are unfamiliar with the particular unit they are using, have them instruct you in its use, and ask lots of questions, check out the scrubber medium, probably sodasorb and ask the people who have been using the gear if it has any particular good points or bad ones.

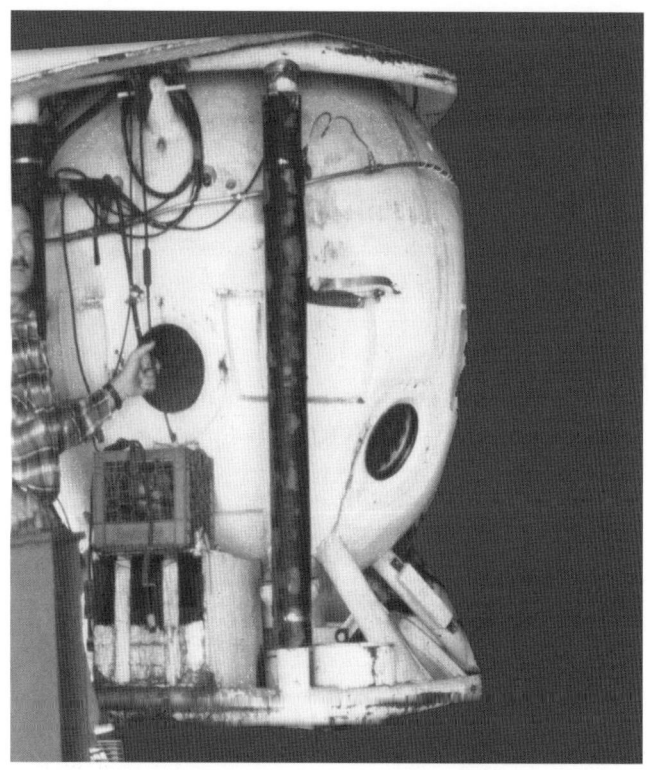

figure 7- Personnel Transfer Capsule (PTC) diving bell.

You may not have your own diving bell with you, and so you will of necessity use theirs. You should be versed in the Federal Regulations, Shipping, Book 46, pages 394 through 409 for your own health.

DO NOT participate in any experimental operations of diving gear or decompression table theories as guinea pig unless your last will and testament is made out and your insurance is paid up.

Examples that come to mind of the perils to guinea pigs (in human form) include that of a former diving contractor in New Orleans who sponsored experiments in a faster means of decompression than what the Navy tables allow. Participants in these experiments were Tenders who, it being wintertime when offshore work is at a standstill, thought they were advancing the cause of science, at five bucks an hour. The only one of these Tenders that I knew personally, whose name I will not use, told me that getting the bends at least once was part of the experiment. Later, when he started diving, he was so susceptible to the bends that he was viewed as a liability, and so the demise of his intended career. The contractor? Persons unknown put five fatal .45 slugs through him in Mexico City, in more recent times. He was on vacation, flashing a lot of money around.

But meanwhile, this writer free-lanced work with virtually every diving contractor (there are a few, big and small, I would avoid) along the Gulf coast. So it was that I was called to do some deep work for a contractor out of New Orleans, one that I was unfamiliar with. At our first meeting, he told me frankly that he was hiring me to replace one of his 'regular' divers, one that had been getting the bends with increasing regularity. Personally, I have thus far never had the bends, although I have felt, what they say, 'dirty' at times. It did not occur to me that this contractor might be using those same experimental tables, faster than the Navy's — if not faster than a speeding bullet — that had screwed up my friend, the guinea pig. But, that was the deal. Hurry UP!

Out on the job a few days later, I met the R.O. (Rack Operator who is in charge of the decompression schedule) and still never thought to look at the decompression tables he was using until we had to drag one diver up the ladder, he was so bent when he reached the surface. We carried him to the decompression chamber, for his long stay on a treatment table. The bends treatment table returned him to all appearances of well-being, but who can say what bit of permanent damage may have been done to each diver, every time they used those experimental tables on each dive, whether or not the effects were immediately noticeable, as in this case?

Another contractor, once the largest of all commercial diving companies in the world, developed headgear that would radically reduce helium consumption by a push-pull breathing system that, while still in the experimental stage, unfortunately exhaled a guinea pig human down its tubes. So, they worked the bugs out, so they thought, and sent it offshore on a job, where it ate another diver. Ooops.

SO, THEY WORKED THE BUGS OUT, SO THEY THOUGHT, AND SENT IT OFF-SHORE ON A JOB, WHERE IT ATE ANOTHER DIVER.

More recently I was told that yet another contractor had acquired this same devour-diver machine, having no doubt (?) finally worked the bugs out, and was touting it as a great money-saver in advertising their services. Science marches on the bodies of guinea pigs.

3.

PLANNING YOUR DIVE
Dedicated to Dan Ditto, Morgan City

Should it happen that you are delegated to dive before you have done a turn as standby diver or diver radio operator, you may have little or no information as to the task that you are to perform underwater. But go ahead and get into your dive dress, short of putting on your helmet and hooking up your hose. Talk to the Engineer of the client company, if he is on deck, and to the supervisor or the radio operator to learn specifics of what has been thus far accomplished, any problems that exist, and confer with the last diver to come up, and ask for his views, and where the tools may be located. Ask to see the radio log, and any drawings or blueprints

figure 8 - Discuss any ideas you may have for completing the task at hand. Converse with the engineer . . .

figure 9- Converse with the tender ...

related to the task to be performed. Discuss any ideas you may have for completing the task at hand, and work for a consensus with the others as to what will be done. Teamwork is the best planning mode.

TEAMWORK IS THE BEST PLANNING MODE

Okay, you know what to do, and your tender has meanwhile put your helmet on the hose, turned on the air to it, and tested the comm', all set, grab the hat and put it on, set the cams and clamp them down.

4. TENDERS

Tenders on river jobs where you will dive into a strong current should wrap the hose around the diver twice before shackling it to the diver's harness, to insure against the shackle accidentally opening, and the taut hose pulling off the divers headgear.

Tenders come in all competence levels from very green to experienced and anxious to 'break out', as the saying goes, and so become a very green diver. But before that event, they will sometimes hold your life in their hands, and their seamanship, perception, or 'weather eye' can make the difference between a productive dive or an accident. Be nice to them.

figure 10-Have the tender wrap the hose around you twice before hooking it to your harness if you are diving in strong current.

You may be a tender one day, or at least relieve them for awhile on holding a hose, give them a break from standing on deck all day.

Tenders will ask the divers for pointers on underwater work, and you'll have a sense of passing along the pointers that at some earlier time were given to you. You should make a point of informing your tender of what you will be doing on your dive, so they may anticipate his/her part in the team effort, which helps you both.

THEIR SEAMANSHIP, PERCEPTION, OR 'WEATHER EYE' CAN MAKE THE DIFFERENCE BETWEEN A PRODUCTIVE DIVE OR AN ACCIDENT.

figure 11 - ***Night dives will soon show you that vision is not often a required element in the work. In murky water, your hands and feet will of necessity provide your 'vision' of the blind.***

figure 12- Tenders are often morose and feel persecuted, which is as it should be, but with both hands tightly holding the diving hose

figure 13- Their language might be Swahili or French Patois.

To have your own tender who regularly works with you is the ideal, but not always possible. Tenders are often morose and feel persecuted, which is as it should be, but with both hands tightly holding the diving hose.

Bailout scuba bottles have saved many lives, including my own, since their use became general in the industry as mandated in the Federal Code of Regulations, Book 46, Shipping, Sect. 197-344. In the next few pages I will describe the death of a diver who would have possibly survived if he had worn a bailout bottle on his last dive. Unfortunately for him, the Fed. Reg.'s did not exist in 1970, years before Divers Local 1012 in New Orleans petitioned the U.S. Congress for Safety Regulations governing commercial diving operations. Before that time, many divers had begun to supply their own bailout bottles, usually no larger than the then-popular 35-cubic foot cylinders. Bigger is better, especially if you're diving deep, or 'live'-boating at any depth. Should your diving hose become entangled in the propeller of the 'live'-boat you are working off of, pinching off your air while reeling you upwards from the sea floor, you'll need the bailout bottles air to break the vacuum created inside your helmet so that you may get out of it before, in a couple of unpleasant ways, it would otherwise be too late.

BAILOUT SCUBA BOTTLES HAVE SAVED MANY LIVES, INCLUDING MY OWN

You should supply your own personal regulator, with an air pressure gauge. I preferred to have the cylinder upside down on my back, with the 2nd stage mouthpiece hung around my neck-dam of the helmet, which would allow me to get air into my neck-dam from below, if I chose. Some individuals connected the bailout directly to their helmets secondary valve connection. I like the option to get out of the helmet entirely, as some situations night require. Make sure the cylinder valve is closed, and that the tender has 'snooped' the fittings for leaks.

5.
WATER ENTRY: LOOK BEFORE YOU LEAP

Preparing to jump, first grab your hose close to where it is shackled or hooked to your harness and give it a hard yank to make sure it is securely connected. Be sure you have enough slack hose over the side for you to reach the water when you jump, and that there are no obstructions or danger of your hose snagging on something and hanging you. Ready? **READY?**

figure 14-Looking for an opening in the floating blanket of stinging jellyfish, you pause. Look before you leap! Note downline tied to rail.

figure 15 - If in doubt, ladders can be climbed both ways.

Wait. If the water is murky and you are the first diver to make this jump, don't jump. Climb down the ladder (another item you need to check, anyway) to assure yourself that you will not break your legs or worse on a pipeline or other item that you cannot see just below the waters surface. This has happened many times.

If you are to establish a down-line when you reach bottom, have it tied to your hose a few feet back, and paid off from a different quarter as you descend.

Okay, everything is set. Gloves on. Clasp knife tied to your harness with a cord long enough for use without untying it. Boot tops taped. Optional chafing gear zipped or buttoned up. Weight belt buckle taped so it does not accidentally pop open, a potential disaster, especially if you are wearing a dry-suit, which could cause you to blow to the surface. A single strip of tape you can easily open. Ready?

Wait. Your comm' (communication) is breaking up. You are standing on the brink, looking through a misting Lexan faceplate at the radio operator who is obviously talking into the radio, but you don't hear anything through your earphones, while the damned 'pot' on your head is starting to weigh a ton.

Take the helmet/hat/pot off your head, figure out what is wrong with the comm', that only moments ago seemed just fine. You, your tender, and the radio operator begin the troubleshooting process of checking the helmet speaker wires, then the comm' studs on the outside of the helmet, then the wires connected to the studs, then the radio end of the wire, and look at the possibility that the radio operator was speaking into the wrong radio, of several diving radios set on the bench of the diving station.

The barge captain, the engineer, and the deck foreman are standing nearby, watching, and the captain looks at his watch. The engineer clears his throat loudly, and the deck foreman begins cursing softly in French patios. Ignore them. But find the problem. Do not get hyper.

The diving supervisor appears with another helmet, and virtually orders you to use it, rather than the one you are familiar with, as a means of clearing up the comm' problem, and getting on with the dive.

If it is a type of headgear that you are unfamiliar with, do not agree to use unfamiliar headgear. Do not succumb to the rush-rush approach to the work that has killed so many, and — in vain attempts to hurry — wrecked equipment, sunk boats, and shut jobs down or put them at a standstill for days, weeks or months. But hurry when you can.

A veteran diver I knew well was killed for having switched to unfamiliar headgear. At the critical moment when he was about to make a dive, his headphones went out, he dove into an emergency situation where he lost comm' with the surface again, indicating that the problem was other than with his own helmet. The radio operator topside signaled the tender to start pulling up on the diver, but the hose was fouled in a davit block, the air pinched off, but they could not know that, with no comm' to the diver. Later, too late, when the standby diver got to him, the diver had suffocated while trying to get the borrowed helmet off his head.

IF IT IS A TYPE OF HEADGEAR THAT YOU ARE UNFAMILIAR WITH, DO NOT AGREE TO USE UNFAMILIAR HEADGEAR. A VETERAN DIVER I KNEW WELL WAS KILLED FOR HAVING SWITCHED TO UNFAMILIAR HEADGEAR

The obvious is to ask the supervisor to give you a crash course in how to get out of the helmet he offers, and ask the tender and radio operator to keep looking for the comm' problem with your hat. Be sure to carry extra speakers with you to the job, and change them out frequently.

If you do lose radio communication during your dive, the universal hand signals used to direct the tender holding your hose are as follows:

> *One* yank or tug on the hose means "I'm okay."
> *Two* tugs mean "Give me slack on the hose."
> *Three* tugs on the hose mean "I'm preparing to leave the sea floor, pick up my slack."
> *Four* tugs on the hose mean "Pick me up."
> *More than four tugs in quick succession on the hose* means "Help, Emergency. Pick me up Now."

Working overseas, I met a supervisor that had broken his legs so badly in a misdirected jump from a barge that they could not allow him to dive anymore, so made him a supervisor. After spending months in a hospital, then supervising for awhile, he had completed his 18-month contract, and went home to learn that his wife had absconded with all the money he had dutifully sent home for 18 months. So it is that I say, in every way,

LOOK BEFORE YOU LEAP!

6.
CURRENTS
Dedicated to Jeff Smith, New Orleans

Be advised that the sea or the river or the harbor or spillway or locks or wakes of a passing ship can generate irresistible strength in their currents, and at 6 knots have a diver stretched out at the end of his hose, blowing like a leaf in a breeze or washed away to who knows where?

Currents at sea can seem to originate out of what was, moments before, a calm, flaccid state.

CURRENTS AT SEA CAN SEEM TO ORIGINATE OUT OF WHAT WAS, MOMENTS BEFORE, A CALM, FLACCID STATE.

figure 16 - An up-ended pipe serves as both a current shield and coffer dam. The shield allows for bottom work by the diver, to include use of the airlift pictured here, which creates another type of current, while dewatering the coffer dam.

figure 17 - A heavily weighted, OSHA-approved toolbasket with a diver aboard is another method to work in strong currents

figure 18 - Final resting place of a jack-up drilling rig, Gulf of Mexico.

I was setting a riser clamp one night on the leg of an oilfield platform, at a location on the leg that was right on the surface of the water, a job that seemed to be easily done without the need of any mask or breathing apparatus. The deck crew standing just above me on the barge handed tools down the ladder to me, and signaled the crane, which was lowering the clamp to me. The ocean was calm, and there was plenty of light from the barge.

Suddenly, hearing a muffled roar off to my right, I looked to see a series of large waves appearing as fast as I can tell it out of the dark and breaking through the underpinnings of the platform, sweeping me off my perch on the clamp and pushing me toward the darkness outside the platform. I was wearing only a wetsuit, and once the waves had passed, I tried to swim back the way I had come, but now there was a strong following current, and headed into the darkness I was swept along with it, passing the last leg. Before I might be lost at sea, I saw something to grab on the leg, and held on until one of the deck hands could throw me a line. A simple lifeline tied to you is worthwhile insurance if you are doing a job on the surface, especially at night, when a tugboat coming out to look for you might more easily run over you than find you.

What I had seen to grab were some barnacles as big as softballs, with the Guardian Angel as pitcher, hmm? I'm delighted whenever I see a barnacle, ever since. But, wear a lifeline. You can never tell when the G.A. might be dozing, lulled by a calm sea.

Tidal currents in San Francisco Bay average about 5 knots, as does the Mississippi River in Spring runoff, complete with cakes of ice and logs coming at you. The Atchafalaya River, deepest in the U.S.A., features a two-way current, one going upstream on the bottom, the other, surface current of course, goes downstream, and either current is 100 feet deep. The mud that these rivers carry make it pitch black the moment your faceplate goes underwater, and any kind of lamp is useless.

Near Cozumel, off of Yucatan in Mexico, is a seaward current that sweeps over the reef and plunges to the depths of the ocean. Some sport-diver friends went scuba diving off the beach there, without knowing of the danger, and one was swept away, never to be seen again, while the two survivors managed to climb, hand over hand, back up the reef and into the shallows before their air ran out. There are undiscovered currents that you may find.

The manmade currents such as are generated by river locks, industrial pumps, ship propellers and the like can be avoided by seeking out the machinery control center and whoever is in charge, and having them shut down everything in the vicinity of where you will be working, and you, personally, and with their guidance, putting tags on each and every one of the shut down control levers or buttons or switches. If you do not happen to have any real tags with you, then some half-sheets of paper with some tape will do the job, with marker pen bold 'DO NOT TOUCH/DIVER DOWN' noted.

The worst scenario: your hose is paid out with you on the end of it, and the tender has not the strength to pull you against the current. Perhaps a rope or a wire, on a large shackle, can be slid down your hose to you, so that you may shackle it into your harness. Or, perhaps there is a crane that can reach you, so to hook into your harness. Be there another pair of hands to help the tender, limit it to no more than two people pulling on a hose. Three people pulling a hose have been known to break it. Ditch your weight belt and surface, lessening the current's pull.

If your hose is fouled, tangled around something where they cannot pull on you from the surface or send you a second line down your hose, consider the 'bailout'. Let's hope that your bailout bottle is independent of your headgear so you may do so. Should it be night, a small, rescue strobe or underwater lamp attached to your harness will make it feasible for them to spot you when you surface, being carried away in the current. Don't panic.

7.
PENETRATION

Diving into any enclosure where there is no route of ascent directly to the surface, if it is more than just a few feet, and perhaps more than one level, should require two backup systems to your primary breathing supply system. You may be going into an enclosure that is too tight for access with the standard bailout scuba backup to be worn, and so might opt to push a bailout bottle ahead of you. In a pinch, your nemo hose might serve as an emergency backup. Don't dive scuba as your primary breathing medium. Your hose is your guideline to the surface, and lack of a guideline has been the death of many novice scuba divers, in deep dark caverns like Jacob's Well near San Marcos, Texas. My information on Jacob's Well is dated, but several years ago I heard that, over time, a dozen divers had died after they got lost and ran out of air in that cavern.

Who knows but what you might one day find yourself in some emergency situation, maybe make a rescue dive into a penetration of a sunken car, boat, or plane, and all you have on hand is a scuba rig. Let's hope you also have a lot of rope to tie to yourself for a vital guideline to find your way out and a sharp knife to cut that rope where it may become tangled in wreckage, and re-tie it.

As much as is possible, refrain from touching the surfaces of the bottom or walls or overhead of the enclosure that you penetrate, due to the silt and mud that coats their surfaces and which will cause your visibility to go zero if you stir it up. Carry a couple of lamps with new batteries, and if you are going far into a vessel or cavern, you might consider placing scuba rigs at intervals along your route of penetration, and perhaps have a backup diver tend your hose from the point where you enter the enclosure.

The bottom line is to know that, after making these efforts at being safe to go where they probably can't pull you up from the surface, to know that you are going to be paid in an amount satisfactory to you for exposing yourself to this additional hazard. Get a consensus of opinions before you commit, and rehearse everybody who will be involved with the dive before you enter the water. If you are required to open a port or hatch, be sure there is not a vacuum or other hazard to be encountered when you open it, and avoid pockets of air that may harbor harmful bacteria.

I submitted a plan to the Army Corps of Engineers, to make a diagonal penetration of submerged tunnel to reach a depth of 400 feet, while actually traversing a distance of 600 feet, first the depth to the tunnel entrance at 150 feet, then 450 feet down the tube, I would station a diver at the tunnel entrance to tend the video robot's umbilical, and keep it from snagging the edge of the 40-foot diameter tunnel entrance, while I would control the rental robot, using a 'joy stick' control and monitor, on the surface.

There are fools who would murder the robot for the privilege of risking their own skin to make this dive, for the money and the glory, mixed with suicidal tendencies. Don't take this person with you to do a penetration dive project.

The Army Corps loved the plan, and promised to call, when they had funding for the job. At the time, the Govt. was spending all its money on Star Wars, and I'm still waiting for the call, which is another of the experiences to be learned in the underwater business.

Consider the two Chinese divers who un-dogged a hatch on a sunken cargo vessel, deep within the bowels of the ship. The compartment within was still full of air, resulting in a suction that killed both divers. Two English divers in scuba were lost in a similar way when they took the plug from the end of a large pipeline in the North Sea. Where any such doubt may exist, drilling, or burning a very small hole through a bulkhead or hatch may save your life. Any hole that you make should be no larger than a small coin, and don't get

WHERE ANY SUCH DOUBT MAY EXIST, DRILLING, OR BURNING A VERY SMALL HOLE THROUGH A BULKHEAD OR HATCH MAY SAVE YOUR LIFE.

too close to any such hole. The suction that can be generated by such vacuums often occur like a series of belches, and may not be immediately noticeable. Give it time, at least a few minutes, and make your drill holes high enough to tap the areas where you *think* there might be large air pockets.

Plate 5-Lowering a jet sled to the pipeline,

Plate 6-And the boss said "watching the damned fish is not conducive to getting anything done. Do you read me? Hey, do you read me?

Plate 7-Coming up free is necessary sometimes. Some jobs finish with a last dive to turn loose the davits, crane line, down-line, etc., leaving nothing up which you might climb. You might sit on your hose like a swing while looking up for the hang-off bar to do your water stops.

Plate 8-It occurred to you, just as you shoot yet another eel, that this thing you have for the underwater might generate some other groceries . . . maybe dive for pay, maybe hardhat, oilfield, or wow, treasure . . . hm. . . golf balls? Change. Time for a diet change.

8.

OILFIELD:

JACKET/PLATFORM PLACEMENT
Dedicated to Lee Brown, Morgan City

Offshore platforms, called 'jackets' when they are newly constructed and without yet having housing, or any of the other functional equipment of the oilfield set upon them, are strong and durable manmade islands.

figure 19 - *Derrik/Gantry crane (above right) setting platform seen through boom of 90-ton crane in foreground.*

figure 20 - *Jacket launching*

figure 21- Jacket under tow to launch site.

figure 22- A blaze of lights from the boom of a derrick crane lights up your dive.

Most often the key to their location, or where they will be placed, is the earlier drilling by either a jack-up or a semi-submersible drilling rig or drill ship, and the submerged oil wells that their efforts have established on the sea floor.

So it is that these bare-bone structures, the jackets, are loaded aboard large floating barges, and towed to designated offshore locations from the shipyards where the jacket fabrication was done. Once on location, these jackets, which are made of heavy and large diameter piping, will be slid off the barge into the sea, where they will float, the sections of pipe being full of air, and sealed. A derrick crane aboard your barge will be hooked to the top of the jacket, and the divers will then guide the jacket, as valves are opened to vent the air so that it sinks, down to the wellheads on the sea floor. Now the jacket is hanging just above the wellheads.

If the seas are running more than 3 feet high, there will be an effect like a pendulum swinging the jacket around, from the rock and roll of the derrick barge as translated to the end of the derrick crane's boom, where the roll will be greater. Seas higher than 3 feet should suspend the operation, pending calmer conditions. The possibility of breaking off a wellhead should urge caution.

It's your turn to dive, and 3-foot seas are acceptable, so here you go. You'll have a lot of swimming to do, so you wear fins. Just before you look, then leap, your tender brings you a roll of thick nylon rope, taped once through the roll with duct tape, so you don't get wound up in it on your swim. You hit the water. You have to swim about 40 yards out to where the top of the jacket hangs from the derrick crane, then down another 140 feet, to the top of one of the two wellheads. The jacket has four decks.

IT'S YOUR TURN TO DIVE, AND 3-FOOT SEAS ARE ACCEPTABLE, SO HERE YOU GO. YOU'LL HAVE A LOT OF SWIMMING TO DO

46 DIVER

Passing under the bottom deck of the jacket, you spot the wellheads standing in their freshly painted, bullet-shaped 'protectors', made of 20-foot pipes with a pointed top on each of them, like two downsized Washington Monuments jutting up from the seabed, 25 feet high.

One is slightly taller, you notice, and head for that one. Reaching its pointed top, you pull one end of the rope loose, and tie it securely to the wellhead's protective cover.

Next, you swim upward, with the other end of the rope, toward the underside of the jacket's bottom deck. You are looking for two holes, called 'bellguides', that are to match the two wellheads when the jacket is lowered over them.

You spot them easily, two round holes the size of manhole covers with light shining down through them into the gloom. Swimming up through the one designated for the taller wellhead, you tie the guide rope to a padeye (metal ring) nearby.

Now, you will have to swim back down the bellguide, leaving your rope tied where it is, and swim out from under the bottom of the deck, then back to where your rope is tied to the padeye, on the top surface of the deck. That will clear your hose, THEN you guide the jacket down over the wellheads.

The rope you have tied between the wellhead and the bellguide is, of course, your guideline for doing this.

From here on, you will be talking to the crane, who will follow your instructions to 'thread the needle'. There's something of a Freudian nature to this particular job, sex with major tinker-toys.

PIPELINE CONSTRUCTION

Santa Fe Marine, an offshore construction firm based in Louisiana developed a new concept for laying pipelines across the sea floor in the early 1970's.

This new concept required the pipelines to be fabricated in large sections ashore, with these sections being welded together, one at a time, as each section in turn was rolled around very large spool drums mounted on the stern of Santa Fe's lay barges. Later, far at sea, the lay barge would unroll the pipeline from the revolving spool, while straightening it. However, pipeline of a larger than 8-inch diameter proved to be too brittle to spool up like thread. The Jay Ray McDermott Company specialized in laying larger diameter pipelines, and the construction and placement of offshore platforms on a scope that is worldwide. To facilitate this, McDermott established an in-house diving division, and have employed many of the best working divers in the far-flung oceans of the world.

The mix of nationalities on many foreign pipeline jobs on one or another of McDermott's lay barges or dredge barges does some good in distracting oneself from the monotony of routine.

Personally, diving work on a (pipeline) lay barge seemed a better job than what any of the 'topside' people had to weather. . . and 'weather' is a key word, because, be it the tropics or the North Sea, they all had to be at their station for their daily 12 hour shift. The divers, on the other band, would in some instances work round the clock several rotations until an underwater pipeline repair was completed, or an especially difficult riser or subsea tie-in was fin-

figure 23 - *Do not stow away on a pipe-laying barge. It is not the Royal Caribbean.*

ished. With any luck, there would follow some time in days to recoup and refit, before the 'divers on deck' summons would be heard again.

Lay barge welders are paid damned good wages, and deserve better, for having the touch to do the precision welding required to join length after length of pipe, a length being called a 'joint' of pipe, usually 40 feet long, and as wide as 60 inches in diameter, watching that arc fire from their torch as they make pass after pass with it for 12 hours.

Pipeline production at the welding stations aboard the lay barge (see illustrations) has sometimes four welding stations in-line adding perhaps 160 feet to the pipeline every hour; the lay barge pulls ahead on its anchors (which are constantly being picked up and advanced by an attendant tugboat) so allowing the pipeline to slide off the barge stern, down through the stinger to settle on the sea floor.

figure 23 - *The pipeline goes down the cradle of the stinger (two parallel, pipelike pontoons) and into the water, angling slowly to the seabed.*

figure 23 - *At the welding stations, 40-ft. lengths (joints) of pipe are added constantly to the pipeline as the pipe lay barge pulls itself along on its anchors, which are reset time and again by attendant tugboats.*

'Stinger' denotes what is actually a pontoon system which, when partially flooded by opening the appropriate valves to admit seawater to the various pontoon tanks, will angle downward from the stern of the lay barge, in order to control the angle of the heavy pipeline as descends to the sea floor in order to prevent bending or breaking it. The stinger as seen on the preceding page is not yet flooded, and the pipeline in its center is nearly to the end of the stinger, almost ready for a diver to attach a cable from the end of the pipeline to one of the legs of the platform seen in the picture. Once this is done, the lay barge will begin to pull away from the platform, and flood the stinger so that the pipeline will angle downward to the sea floor.

During the days and nights that follow, divers will periodically make inspection dives, diving scuba in the 'buddy' system, to note the configuration of the pipe to the stinger and sea floor. A plastic slate and grease pencil are the working tools. This inspection 'bounce' dive is often a good depth pay and an invigorating swim, unless you use a scooter, which you may have to rescue. Watch the currents, and perhaps employ an 'octopus' of more than one second stage. If you have to make an emergency ascent out past the end of the stinger, you are a long ways from home.

PIPELINE
DREDGING AND JET SLEDS
Dedicated to Dave McCallister, Morgan City

" . . .Dreamed I would then an
    Ocean Farmer be
    But instead I am a ditch-digger
    at the bottom of the sea "— Vance Johnson, 1968

Jet Sleds such as the one pictured in Plate 5 are machines developed to dig ditches at the bottom of the sea. The diver, here shown as he hangs on to a high part of the sled, guides the crane by use of his radio communication, to where the sled will straddle the pipeline. Often, a buoyed rope that is tied to the pipeline will be used to help guide the sled, with the diver seeing by the downward angle of the rope which way to maneuver. This rope is vital in murky water, or at night.

Offshore pipelines are comparatively fragile tubes, when compared to a ships anchor, or the deep-draft keel of some boats, or the power of a shrimp boat that snags an exposed pipeline with its net while running at high rpm's. So it is that law requires pipelines to be buried, after an inspection diver has traversed the pipeline itself, to make sure that no damage to it happened during the construction phase described in the last chapter.

Once the jet sled is set, its runners paralleling the pipe on either side in a straddling position, it will be secured to the pipe itself, and the work of digging a ditch under the pipe will begin. There are several designs and variables in the hardware of jet sleds, some are self-propelling, some are towed along the pipeline by the jet or dredge barges. Some are as light as a couple of tons, and others as heavy as 25 tons, and so I will not go into describing nomenclature here which might not fit the particular sled that you may work with. Suffice to say, all jet sleds in my experience employ high-pressure water jet nozzles positioned to blast mud, sand and boulders loose and away. Following close behind the hp jet nozzles are one or more airlifts that suck out these items, and blow it off to either side of the sled as it progresses along the pipeline. Thus, a ditch is dug and conveniently, under the pipeline, itself. A diver must avoid the hazards of these earth-moving devices, or effectively be plucked, sucked, and spit out along with the mud of the ditch.

By the time you may be working with a jet sled you will probably have done your share of digging with use of a high-pressure hose, using either a 'T' nozzle, or dolphin nozzle, either of which are built with balanced water jets in their design, so as to avoid you being blown around as would be the case with a standard fire-hose nozzle.

With a jet sled, there will be clusters of such nozzles, and the pressure blasting out of them will be three times that of a jet hose. Do not dive in a mask when you work on a jet sled. They have been known to be blown off of a diver's head by a sled's nozzles.

The ideal situation is that you are able to see the jet sled before it is submerged, and so climb around on it and take notes. If not, and you will be making a dive on it, probably while it is running, you will be able to see little or nothing on bottom. Prepare for this dive as outlined in the section on 'Planning Your Dive' by having a drawing made to show the location where the divers down-line is tied to the sled, and the 'safe' route to follow while inspecting the jet sled. While working on a sled that is running, if at any time you feel that you are disoriented, lost, or in the wrong place, then have the tender pull you up until you can get back on the down-line, and start over.

IF AT ANY TIME YOU FEEL THAT YOU ARE DISORIENTED, THEN HAVE THE TENDER PULL YOU UP UNTIL YOU CAN GET BACK ON THE DOWN-LINE, AND START OVER.

If the work is in otherwise clear water, you may be able to see the sled, or a cloud of billowing mud below you where it is digging, as you descend the down-line toward the sled. Take a look at the high-pressure hoses that conduct the air and water to it on your way down. See if from where you are on the down-line you can see any evidence of a leak or any other problems with those HP hoses, and if so, report it immediately to the surface.

Jet sleds generally move only a few feet per minute, and may be digging a ditch 9 feet deep under the pipeline. You will be taking nemo fathometer readings in your periodical inspection dives, once the jet sled is set on the pipeline and running. You will make these inspections in bounce dives, until you have gone into a decompression requirement. There will be an air of competition to see who can do the fastest inspection of the sled.

Hurry when you can, but make sure you do a thorough inspection. If it turns out that you notice that the sled is not working properly, as sometimes happens, then you are doing what you are paid for, rather than setting a speed record.

A diver I worked with was so hurried that be failed to open the sled 'doors', which held it to the pipeline, when be was sent to detach the sled so it could be picked up. The sled bent the pipeline into a large bow, some 15 feet above the seabed. Such a snafu is very difficult to repair. Gain competence, then try for increased speed at a given task. If you like rodeos, you'll love the up and down plunges of a jet sled as you lower it toward setting it on a pipeline. Take some coaching before you do this first time.

RISER CONSTRUCTION

A riser by definition is a vertical section of pipe that, in oilfield application, connects to a pipeline that is on the seabed. The riser will normally be clamped to one of the platform legs or other of the platform underpinnings, such as horizontal or diagonal braces.

Simply stated, diving procedure is, first you put the clamps on the leg (or other locations as required), which requires cleaning of the sea growth from the areas designated for each clamp to be set, then the clamp is bolted together on the leg, and left loose enough so that it can be moved around the leg. The diver pictured is push-kicking open the leg clamp, which is 'hinged' on one side by three bolts loosely set in the 'ears' of the clamp. Note the other clamp already in place above the diver.

Next, once the clamps are in place, a measurement will be taken from the end of the pipeline on the seabed to the inside-back 'saddle' of the smaller, riser part of the bottom clamp, as shown in the picture in Plate 6 of this book.

If you make the dive to take the measurement, I suggest using a length of small-gauge copper wire, one that you can either cut or tie a knot in, to mark the ends of your measurement.

This done, there will then be a dive made to attach the crane line to the pipeline. The crane will then raise the pipeline to the surface, where a riser will be welded to it, in a welding station hastily setup on the side of the barge by the pipeline welders.

Important to your dive while setting the clamps is to note exactly how the clamp is rigged by the deckhands, before it goes in the water on a crane or air-tugger wire. It should hang straight, when lifted, since clamps are very heavy, and if it is cocked, may cause problems. Once the riser has been welded onto the pipeline, you may be required to set the riser in the bottom clamp, which is standard procedure. Once the bottom of the riser, close to where it is welded to the pipeline, is set in the bottom clamp by your directing the crane while it lowers the riser to you, the job is finished, except that there will be some additional juggling to put the full length of the riser in all the clamps up to the surface of the water.

Tenders are often given a chance to dive to tighten, and tighten, and tighten until the impact wrench won't tighten the clamps anymore.

PIGS IN THE PIPE

As standby diver one morning, watching the bubbles from a working diver below pop languidly on the surface and basking in the reflected sunlight off the new, freshly painted jacket that our barge was tied up to, I offered to take the diver's hose from the tender so that he might get us some coffee from the galley. The diver, who was our most experienced tender, was tightening the bolts on one of the last riser clamps to be finished up, some 30 feet below. The top of the riser, an open 8-inch pipe, protruded from the calm surface of the water, close to the edge of the barge where we stood.

As the tender started to hand me the hose, there came a loud hiss of rushing air from the open top of the riser, then a loud bang, like a cannon shot, as a rubber pig shot from the riser, and bounced off the jackets top deck into the sea.

figure 26 - Hi-tech pig employed to inspect 40-inch oil transport pipeline. This particular pig incorporates ultrasound and other electronic measuring devices to determine the effects of electrolysis and corrosion on the submerged pipeline.

We had both made a standing jump of several feet across the deck, but he had not let go of the hose.

"Hey, why're you jerking on my hose?" came the tired voice from the diving radio.

"Frightened by a pig," answered the radio operator. "Come back on that?" queried the diver, in a perplexed tone.

Now I took the hose so that the tender might enjoy a dip in the sea, to rescue the pig.

Pig sizes come in all pipe diameters, and are propelled through pipelines by compressed air. Most often this is the last phase of pipeline construction, to assure the pipeline owners that there is no obstruction to the passage of materials through it. With new pipelines a 'dumb' pig will be used, made of hard rubber, with a sonic pinger set inside of it. In case it does get stuck somewhere inside the line, more diving work will be required.

Most often, there will be a 'pig trap' connected to the end of a pipeline, probably a steel cage of some sort. In the case of the hi-tech pig shown on the preceding page, a cradle with overhead detachable iron bars is bolted onto the end of a submerged pipeline by divers, with a crane line attached to it. When the pig arrives, it will be picked up still in its cradle and placed on deck, for the technicians to ponder.

RIG DIVING

Oilfield drilling rigs are of several types, and this is because of the varying depths of the water they are intended to drill in.

For the shallower, in-shore drilling work there are a variety of jack-up drilling rigs, some of them self-propelled that can be deployed in the coastal waters and bays. Where very shallow work is to be done, there are derricks (the drilling tower made of steel beams) set upon wide, shallow barges that, with use of drag lines and small tugs, can be positioned where there is little or no water interspersed, as in a swamp, or tidal zone. A 'drag line' in this connotation is actually a 'steam' shovel (usually in fact diesel powered) that is most often employed to move the mud and muck necessary to establish the shallow-water drilling rig at its intended location.

Wherever there is any amount of water, divers may be called at some point to assist in either the initial set-up of such a rig, or later, to provide any number of tasks related to the actual drilling process. A drilling template will be placed underwater, and casing pipe will soon follow.

Casing pipe is usually 24 inches in diameter, in 40-foot lengths. The drilling template is like a large, steel plate with holes in it called 'bell guides', as illustrated in Plate 3, 'Threading the needle'. Once the drilling template is in place, then the casing pipe is raised on end, a piece at a time, and is driven down through the bell guides into the mud, establishing a sort of vertical pipeline, through which the drill-bit and 'stinger' of drill-pipe will follow, to begin the actual drilling. Later, a BOP (blow-out preventer) will be lowered, which is a massive steel device that is intended to contain the high pressures that may be tapped when the drill penetrates a pocket of oil or gas.

Where jack-up drilling rigs are concerned, divers will often be required to make bottom surveys preceding the actual drilling to insure that the (usually three) legs of the jack-up platform are solidly set on the sea floor and to clear any obstructions to this initial set-up of the rig.

One or more sweeps of the bottom, especially in the area where the drilling template is to be located, will be made, and this procedure may take several days. People throw a lot of trash into the sea.

One of the dangers to possibly be encountered in this rather mundane task is that of stainless steel wire entanglements, especially if the drilling rig is a stationary platform, such as are often established on the location after a jack-up rig makes the initial discovery of oil. Stationary drilling platforms are discussed under the heading, 'Jacket/Platform Placement'.

When a stationary platform is established, there may follow many years of successive stages of work on that platform, and, with platform rigs that have been over wellheads for years, there is likely to be an accumulation of wire, steel beams, hoses and pipe and any number of items such as are discarded by the platform over time.

These oilfield junkyards can be hazardous to divers, in the form of crusty steel edges that can cut, and wire and piping that can entangle you and your hose. Often, in doing bottom sweeps under stationary rigs, your hose will pass over and around obstructions that will not allow the tender who handles your hose to pull on you. You must keep yourself free of the junk, while moving through it.

The truly deep-water drilling rigs are those known as semi-submersibles, massive skyscrapers set on high, vertical cylinder pontoons like stilts, which can be flooded and sunk to a prescribed depth to stabilize the rig at sea. There, perched and floating on deep water, the anchors of the semi-submersible will be set by their attendant buoy tender, usually a large oilfield workboat with giant winches aboard. Sometimes it will be necessary for a diver to work from the buoy tender to assist the buoy tender in picking up a semi-submersible's anchors.

I know of one accident in which a buoy tender's winch actually pulled the boat underwater, with the loss of seven crewmen, in a freak combination of high seas coming over the stern into open chain lockers while the boat was engaged in picking up one of a semi-submersible's anchors. The surviving captain said that his first inkling that they were going down was when the water came through the wheelhouse, the highest part of the boat's superstructure.

There have been several jobs during which I was reluctant to get out of my dive dress between dives, and working a buoy tender in rough seas is one of them. A wetsuit is better than a life jacket, any day or night.

Another of the deep-water drilling rigs is the drill ship, which is just that, a ship with a drilling derrick tower set amidships. Such ships are usually equipped with moon-pools, saturation systems, even submarines for extremely deep-water drilling. Their computerized positioning systems often don't work that well in high seas, and may bonk you with a diving bell.

Both semi-submersibles and drill ships have been lost in storms at sea, and jack-up rigs have been toppled and sunk by gas blowouts. There is no guarantee when technology gets into a wrestling match with mother nature, witness the Titanic, or the Edmond Fitzgerald, the Triple Crown, or Penrod 53. The list goes on, from ancient times through tomorrow. The sea gives, and takes away.

> **THERE IS NO GUARANTEE WHEN TECHNOLOGY GETS INTO A WRESTLING MATCH WITH MOTHER NATURE**

With dynamic positioning systems, such as are incorporated in many large dive boats and ships, anchor winches aboard those vessels are synchronized by computer to pick up and slack off the anchor chains in sequence to compensate for the currents or high seas that may assault a vessel while it is located over some task that is being conducted by divers on the sea floor below the vessel.

Diving in this mode will be done through moon-pools, large wells situated through the decks and hull of the vessel, allowing diving bells to be lowered and picked up through these wells without as much banging and hazard as with deploying the bell over the side of a vessel. Dynamic positioning is more effective in centering a moon-pool than it would be otherwise.

But if the seas become too rough, the divers may be subjected to a dangerous game of 'tag' with a heavy diving bell swinging around their workplace. In that situation, it is time to shut down the work, pending calmer seas.

It is not unusual for any drilling rig, from the swamp to the deep blue waters of the ocean, to have on board a full time diver, just in case.

Drilling rigs may work for weeks or months without tasks for a diver, but still have one aboard, especially if the rig is located abroad, in some trackless sea, far from the underwater labor pools like those of New Orleans or Santa Barbara, California.

One diver I heard about was stationed on a rig in the North Sea for three months, and then it developed that some diving was going to be done, and a crew of several other divers was slated to arrive for this event, which was to employ a mini saturation diving system in deep water. The diver who had been on the rig for those three months, upon learning that a dive was going to be made, promptly quit his job. It was later speculated that he was an imposter, someone who had no diving experience whatever.

Such are the rigors of rig diving. You may play chess and checkers and tire of eating steak dinners and watching endless bloody videos and play cards and run out of books and review the videos again . . . and again.

Diving down on a sunken drilling rig, a jack-up Penrod drilling rig off the coast of Texas, I could see that there had been some excitement aboard the rig when it took its plunge to the bottom.

A high-pressure blowout had occurred, when they unexpectedly hit a pocket of natural gas under such pressure that it first threw all the pipe and casing up out of the hole, opening the way for a blast of gas-borne mud and sea water that spun the huge rig around on its axis, tearing off one of the three legs and toppling the whole rig over into a large, moonlike crater that the blast had opened in the sea floor.

The crew of the jack-up had evacuated the rig before the blowout, thanks to the telltale signs that such a calamity was about to happen having been noticed by one of the crew, who spread the alarm.

Where drilling rigs are employed in U.S. waters, there will be no 'rig diver' aboard, and when they need somebody, your pager goes off. We've about gone full circle to the first chapter, except that there are some other things particular to rig diving that you should be aware of.

Here's an example. You and your mates arrive aboard Driller X, let's say, in the Gulf of Mexico. You get picked up to the rig from the pitching deck of a crew boat, swung high in the air while clinging to a personnel basket, and set down gently on the broad steel deck of the jack-up rig.

Divers and tenders set up the dive station, you store your gear, and then are graced with a visit from the rig superintendent. You are to dive down and connect three cable slings, using shackles, to a drilling template they intend to pick up and set on deck.

The dive supervisor, your boss, says 'You dive first.' So you go get in your gear. The diving station is your next stop, and it is located on the underside of the rig, down a flight of stairs, called a 'ladder' in swab vernacular. You'll be working on bottom, so you're wearing boots.

When you get to the diving station deck, you look over the big, steel bucket they are going to lower you to the water with. You cut about 40 feet of rope and tie it to the side of the bucket. Supervisor asks, "What's that for?" "So I can find my way around," you say. He tries to tell you that you won't need the search rope. You kind of wonder about this guy. You're new here, and you don't know anybody.

The wire slings are hanging above you, by the same crane that is going to pick up the template, once you rig the slings to it. You climb into the bucket, which seems a little tipsy. One end of the search rope is tied to the bucket, and you tie the other end to your harness. You take your helmet from the tender, put it on and clamp it down on your neck-dam.

Comm' checks out okay . . . . Who is this 'Roger, Roger', anyway . . . . ?

The small overhead winch begins its creaking turns that lower you and the bucket downward toward the dark, wind-whipped sea. It is 0300 hours. The surface of the Gulf is choppy, and as the bucket gets to the water surface, you are hit by a couple of waves. The bucket stops, and you get creamed by a couple more waves, while you make inquiries as to what the hell is happening? Get me on bottom!

They reply, rather casually, that it is not known whether there is enough wire cable in the small winch to get you to the sea floor, some sixty feet deep. You get plowed by another wave as you suggest that they lower the bucket far as it will go, or at least, below the surface.

Under the waves at last, you strongly suggest that they keep an eye on the winch cable to see if it will get you to the bottom. Finally, you're there. You climb out in the darkness, flick on your lamp, but the turbulence is so great, even sixty feet down, that the lamp only throws reflected, blinding light off the sand particles, and you turn it off. Wave surges at this depth? A first time for everything.

Making sure that your air hose is not fouled on the bucket, you head out across the template with the end of one of the heavy slings, having the crane lower it as you advance into solid blackness.

YOU CLIMB OUT IN THE DARKNESS, FLICK ON YOUR LAMP, BUT THE TURBULENCE IS SO GREAT...

Your search line is all played out, tugging where it's tied to your harness, and you still have found noth . . . . wait, there it is. You cut the search line to save untying it, and begin shackling the wire sling to a padeye (see chapter on Jacket/Platform Placement), and following the sling back to the other end on the crane hook, you select another sling and begin groping around in the dark for another padeye on the template to shackle the sling to. Blip, blam, you've got the three slings rigged as ordered to the three equal points of the template.

Okay, you say, pick me up when I get in the bucket. They say (it's that weird supervisor) wait, you have to change the slings around, re-rig it, put one sling where another one is, take that sling and. . .

You're thinking that the template is an even triangle, from the drawings you saw. The slings are of equal length, spreading out to the three corners of the template. What's to re-rig? "Just do it," he says.

"Roger, Rogerrr . . . ." You intone the magical words, while you busy yourself in searching, your hands reaching about in the darkness, for the search line you had cut earlier. Crossing over the slings that they now want you to change around, you crisscross the template. The bucket is not there.

Your bottom time is running out, and the bucket is your only way, your elevator back up to the rig's deck, some fifty feet above the sea. The supervisor begins counting down the last ten minutes in your ear, in 5-second increments.

"Shut up, please," you say politely, "and tell me where the bucket is." The supervisor tells you it is on the surface, and goes back to his countdown dramatics. He's doing what he can to drive you nuts.

Three dive teams, 6 men to connect 3 slings to a template, you think, while working hurriedly to rotate them as ordered. "Ours not to question why . . ." And you are finished, with 30 seconds to go.

You tell them to pick you up, and the bottom-surge helps in this, lifting you up in its current, even as you feel the tender begin pulling on your hose. The current buffets you around as you are lifted upward, and you turn on your lamp again, off bottom, so that they may see you when you reach the surface.

Breaking surface, rough swells lift you high and plunge you down as you look around for the bucket. You see it but you cannot swim against the current to reach it, and they cannot move the bucket to you where you are dangling on the end of your hose. What to do?

You are about to suggest lowering both it and yourself to thirty feet below the surface, when you spot the search line. Streaming out from where it is tied to the bucket, like help, reaching for you. Gratefully you grab it, and, pulling your way to the bucket, you climb into it. Home free!

But not quite. On the way up, the sling holding the bucket slips, and you are almost dumped out. Finally having gained the deck, you drop your weight belt, pop off your helmet, quickly hand it to the supervisor, and head for the shower. Once there, with the hot water blasting away your hypothermia, you reflect on the hour just passed. Easy money. You smile at the thought.

9. ATTITUDE ADJUSTMENTS

Commercial diving work often requires us to be alone in an alien environment where the stakes are high, and unlike most occupations the loner is here more in his/her element than in most jobs.

Although there are a lot of singular individuals in this work, it is those who put aside the absolute loner of their makeup to participate in a team effort that are able to learn and grow in the trade. We all like to excel as individuals, and there is ample opportunity for that in underwater projects where we each make our dive alone, in succession, one after the other, as the Rotation List may dictate.

Your call to go on standby may come at 1500 hours in the midafternoon, or at 0300 hours in the dark of early morning. You may be required to first operate the diving radio(s), keeping both the decompression schedules for a diver making water-stops on his way up from the bottom, while keeping track of another diver who has just entered the water and will be working at three different depths before starting their ascent. If the diving requires mixed gas, probably Heliox, you may be required to serve as Rack Operator in rotation, monitoring the flow of breathing mix to the diver, and while keeping track of the bottom time, in effect, the decompression schedule, and all the while directing the crane by relaying the diver's radio commands.

It is vital to the work and the safety of all concerned and your reputation and future in the diving business to be on the level. First of all, do not get hyper. Stay calm. If coffee gives you the jitters, avoid it, unless you are becoming very tired, in which case it may only restore your focus. Focus is what you need, in this line of work.

Everybody screws up, while trying not to. You must admit your mistakes, and grow by them. Double-check your paperwork while figuring decompression schedules if they are new to you, and never try to memorize the U.S. Navy Diving Decompression tables, but always refer to your copy of that text.

If, on your dive, you lost some tool that is vital to the work at hand, report it immediately and resolve to tie or tape such a tool to yourself in future dives. Do not let the next diver waste a lot of time trying to find a tool that is not there, or worse, feel that they have to cover for your mistake. Nobody likes a 'snitch', or informer, but you have to weigh the consequences of covering for someone who may, at some point, try to blame it all on you.

figure 27 - Avoid that headache.

There are enough headaches to deal with in any industrial workplace without adding to them with the snowballing effect of lying to save face. As a supervisor in my own time, I was impressed when a diver would have the foresight to admit a mistake in the work when it might not have been otherwise obvious that something was amiss, and so a remedy could be immediately implemented.

Unless someone is caught in a lie, or they are recognized as incapable of maintaining safety concerns such as are first priority on any job, I would not penalize them for honesty. Honesty in the workplace should be rewarded, and these are the people who can interact and make the team effort that makes overall success so much easier, benefiting each individual who pulls for team effort.

10.
DAM DIVING

Hydroelectric and Flood Control dams provide the diver with some of the best work that could be imagined. The water is often deep, and very cold, since there are no currents except for the manmade variety of sluices, pinstocks, and spillways that would not be operating or moving the turbines while diving operations are in progress.

Such dams exist in every nation of the world. The dams of the world are often located in mountainous settings, backing up rivers that fill deep canyons. Often, these canyons have many miles of

figure 28 - Parker Dam, Colorado River, Arizona.

figure 29 - Stainless steel bulkhead just prior to lowering through keyway of barge to the upstream opening of a pinstock (pipeline going through the dam) in order to plug it.

figure 30 - Roosevelt Dam, constructed by imported Italian stonemasons and Apache Indians around the turn of the century, provides water and power for Phoenix, Arizona.

shoreline, along underwater slopes that vary from gentle angles to sheer cliffs that plunge to 500 feet and more. The lakes that are thus created are of water that never moves, receiving little sunlight, due to the terrain of surrounding mountains. The water is numbing cold, dry-suit weather.

Diving in Lake Powell, which is backed up by Glen Canyon Dam in northern Arizona, I had contracted to salvage a pleasure boat, and was surprised to find that from the end of the dock on the edge of the lake, the water depth was 160 feet deep, and going down. The elevation of the lake above sea level was several hundred feet, and so diving schedules of decompression were figured with altitude correction tables as applied to the U.S. Navy decompression tables.

With spring runoff, the melting snows then pour their torrents from the mountains into the lakes, sometimes with such volume that the dams may be topped and overrun by the flood. Even with all their spillways and gates wide open, some modern dams have been temporarily relegated to the role of just another waterfall by a river running on nature's agenda. Such floods require intensive underwater inspections and repairs. Video, ultrasonics, and pressure-grouting may be indicated, after the flood subsides.

A byproduct of spring runoff is silt, mud that is transferred from the mountain slopes and valleys to the bottom of the lakes that are backed up by dams. This silt layer grows deeper with each runoff, and some studies have indicated that many of our major dams will eventually be rendered useless by this silting. A diver of my acquaintance was once approached by the FBI who asked him if he could arrange to lower a TV camera to the bottom of Hoover Dam, on the Colorado River, at Lake Mead. It seems that they suspected some fiend of having dropped the weighted bodies of his victims into the lake, from the center of the dam. From his own experience, the diver explained to the FBI that because of the silt layer of varying intensity at the bottom of the dam, visibility was zero for the last hundred feet of the 500-foot depth at the center of the dam. At its top, the silt intensity is so fine that it can hardly be discerned from the water above it, but as an object, be it a camera or a body, is lowered into the silt, it eventually reaches a point where, like water displacement on a boat hull, it can sink no deeper. This pea-soup consistency thickens in subsequent layers to a solid, at the bottom. When working in the silt layer, a diver's breathing regulator may be adversely affected by the clogging aspect of such tiny granules.

Working at Horse Mesa Dam on the Salt River near Phoenix,

Arizona, we were doing long bottom-time dives at a depth of 60 feet while doing repairs on a trash rack. Trash racks are heavy, steel grates that prevent sunken trees, limbs and other large items from entering an intake, in this case, for a large pump. We were utilizing a decompression chamber to do the usual surface portion of our decompression, and then traveling by road over a mountain top to Tortilla Flats, where we were billeted. I felt 'dirty' by the time we got to Tortilla Flats. Like the bends were coming on. Gee, how high is that mountain top? *Message*: You don't need an airplane to get you to a dangerous altitude after a decompression dive. *Solution*: Add decompression, perhaps going to the next deeper table schedule, breathing oxygen. Or, bunk in the chamber.

Some of the things that are particularly gratifying about underwater dam work are the lack of water turbulence, no up and down motion of a crane boom, and the professionalism and safety consciousness of the River Crews, those people assigned to work with the divers, who are employees of the dam system. These people are often hospitable, inviting divers over for elk steaks and the like. When compared to overseas oilfield diving, where the diver may get ashore once every 45 days to find themselves beset by vandals and pursued by cannibals, and perhaps be infected by strange diseases, dam work provides a real break.

I asked Bob Hunter, longtime friend and Director of the T.V.A Diving Division, if he might consider writing a book on dam diving. He replied that they were always learning something new, and so with these few pointers, I refer you to the learning mode.

11. ENVIRONMENTAL DIVING

The harvest of the sea's natural wealth has been ongoing since time began. More recently, petroleum has been added to the cornucopia of that wealth. The problem that mankind has brought to this feast is the imbalance caused by gluttony and carelessness. As with the American Bison, the misguided impression is that a species of fish must exist in limitless numbers. Be they Bluefin Tuna, Rock Cod, Abalone and a long list of others, they are disappearing at an accelerated rate.

Alarmed by this, well-meaning laws are passed to stop or reduce the harvest of some species, both fish and mammal, often resulting in a sudden resurgence of a species along with a growing population of the predators that have always fed on these same fish and mammals. Thus, with a new increased population of California Sea Lions, the natural prey of the Great White Shark, so it follows that there are increased sightings, and attacks on humans, by those now-famous jaws.

I watched, horrified, as the captain of a long-line fishing boat cut the leader line on which a huge Bluefin Tuna was hooked, and the 1,000-pound carcass sink slowly into the depths, until it was gone from sight. We had been checking the miles of fishing line that the boat had strung out, marked by buoys that were the line's floats, from horizon to horizon across the Gulf of Mexico.

By law, this tuna was out of season. Legally, the captain could have been jailed, if caught with the fish on board his boat. As I watched the fish, drowned during its time on the hook, sink out of sight, I thought of the hungry multitudes of this earth. It was a sight I will never forget.

The Pacific Sea Otter is a cute skindiver that eats voraciously of shell fish along the California coast. Now fully protected under law, it has become a common sight to the beachgoer, and it is most often seen while eating, laying on its back as it munches on its prey, in the amber kelp that grows outside the surf line. With no natural enemy but the white shark, this nifty-looking predator has joined his human counterpart in the ongoing decimation of the abalone and other shellfish populations.

In recent times, the abalone populations of Southern California disappeared to such an extent that diving for them (by humans) is illegal. Whether they will reappear in any numbers is a curiosity, given the resurgence of the sea otter population.

figure 31- **Standing in blue, waves golden.**

figure 32- Lobsters at home, Bahama Islands.

In Cayucas, a beach community north of Morro Bay, California, is an abalone 'farm', where the crustacean is being grown in a controlled environment, under the eyes of marine biologists. This is but one facet of the possibilities for those of us who would seek a livelihood in the realm of environmental concerns.

A couple that I am acquainted with have a house set on a cliff, overlooking a cove below, and in the center of the small cove, an ocean inlet of the Pacific, is a sea lion rookery. Often, this rock platform in the middle of the cove will be covered by sea lions of all ages, an almost solid, blubbery carpet with spots of gold color denoting the infant pups among the solid dark brown of the adults.

Into this sea lion paradise one day swam a pod of killer whales, four of them, and they proceeded to surround the rock, which was covered with sea lions. While the couple watched in amazement, the sea lions plunged into the water, forming a tight ball of their bodies, through which the killers plowed, grabbing sea lions in an orgy of blood and carnage. Most of the sea lions escaped, diving to the bottom and heading quickly out to sea.

So would 'natural selection' feed the killers, one might say.

It was once common for fishermen to shoot sea lions on sight, and as a child I recall the stench of their rotting corpses where they had washed ashore, several puncture wounds to be seen would tell the tale of their demise. Fishermen hated sea lions because they invaded their fishing nets, so they shot them any time they saw them.

The couple who had watched the killer whales feast decided they could do something about the shooting of sea lions, and they successfully organized and lobbied the state senate to implement laws protecting sea lions. Some fishermen were outraged.

Within days of the implementing of the new laws, there came another invasion of the cove, this one more deadly than the killer whales.

A fishing boat chugged into the cove below the house, and once again, the sea lions dove into the water, where they were all destroyed by the shock waves created by the dynamite that the fishermen threw into the sea. This act of mad revenge, the thunderclaps of the explosions and the loud epithets that echoed up the cliffs, underline the passions of the warring sides to virtually every issue of conservation. It can be a dangerous calling, the urge to save the planet.

The fishermen? They were jailed and fined, and the couple who lived above the cove, the couple who had this murder done to them in a very real sense, built their fences higher, and hired watchmen to keep an eye on things while they lived abroad for long periods.

Under the protection of the new laws, the sea lion population has grown in such numbers that the white shark, a predator that feeds on them, has also made a significant comeback. You may want to avoid looking like a sea lion, if you can, when you go into the waters along the Pacific coast.

Usually, the white shark will take one bite, and realizing its mistake, will spit the diver out, if that's any consolation.

> **THE WHITE SHARK WILL TAKE ONE BITE, AND REALIZING ITS MISTAKE, WILL SPIT THE DIVER OUT**

One diving contractor that I worked for out of New Orleans had as his client-customer one of the oldest existing underwater oilfields in the Gulf of Mexico. Being one of the first such oilfields, and dating back to the early 1950's, it preceded many of the now in-place laws governing such places. To work this underwater oilfield was to fix leaking pipelines, one after another, daily, and sometimes into the night.

At many places in this field, the seabed was a tangle of interweaving pipelines, a rusting mess of 3, 4 and 6-inch diameter pipe in a spaghetti-like maze, exuding bubbles of black oil to the surface. Often, while repairing a leak in one pipeline, another pipeline would be discovered to be leaking, also. Smith-Plus, Plidco, and Weld-End clamps were the stock of my trade, among others, to try to stem the flow of crude oil into the waters of the Gulf,

figure 33- *Ocean oil well.*

There are many pros and cons in the debate over what long-term effect the loosing of crude oil has on the environment. All I can say for sure is that before oil wells, there were natural seepings of oil into the seas in many places where currently oil wells exist. The oil producers argue that their wells have stemmed natural seepage, by reducing the pressure of those sometimes huge pockets of oil.

On the other hand, one driller hit a large pocket of natural gas off the coast of Mexico in the late 1970's, and, so large and great was the pressure of this well that it blew everything out, and became an open vent by which a steady, roaring geyser of gas blew ongoing for 6 months into the atmosphere. All the king's horses and men, to coin a phrase, could not put a cap on the blowout until barges loaded with large, steel balls deluged it in a mountain of balls.

Before this solution was arrived at, and no doubt the pressure had been reduced somewhat by 6 months of constant blowout, there had been a succession of other attempts to put a lid on it. Three divers lost their lives in these various failures.

A friend in Santa Barbara, California contracted to one of the major oil companies in that oilfield to photograph tiny but very colorful marine animals, called nudibranchs, living, on the underwater areas of their oilfield platforms. Thought to be rare anywhere in the world, these animals were thriving and populous there.

A shellfish much prized for its delicate beauty, the spiny oyster, was unknown in the Gulf of Mexico until the advent of deepwater oilfield platforms, and are numerous in many places on these rigs, where the water depth exceeds 150 feet. Whole fish populations have developed around these rigs; corals, shellfish, and every type of fish inhabit the legs and braces that are festooned with various types of sea growth.

WHOLE FISH POPULATIONS HAVE DEVELOPED AROUND THESE RIGS

Otherwise, the Gulf for the most part has a bottom made of clay, with little nutrient value, necessary to support fish populations. The 'Flower Garden', a natural coral reef off the Texas coast, is the only exception to this that I know of. A popular skindiver destination, whale sharks seem to like the place, and are often photographed with the usual scuba diver holding onto their tail.

Some of the newly emerging nations of the world are perhaps less conscious of the declining environment, and in their rush to get a 'piece of the pie' (before we, the great consumers, get it all) they may tend to run a bit rough-shod on their own environments.

Working offshore of West Africa in the 1970's, I immediately noticed the globules of grease, like petroleum jelly, that were everywhere in the ocean there, in which I worked. But these oilfields belonged to an American company. This company, as with many overseas portions of American companies, was required by their agreement with the host nation to train the local Africans to do the work of the oilfield. Old hands at this sort of work, being human, are known to make mistakes, but where new trainees are concerned, they can wreak havoc. One such mistake by the new trainees was to open a valve that created an oilslick of gigantic proportions, before they realized their mistake.

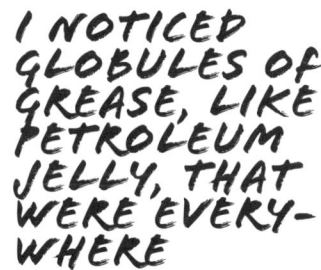

On the other band, some of the old hands, being in the usual oilfield rush to get things done in the hurry-up mode, did things like create the oilspill picture in this chapter by cutting corners that they knew would never be tolerated in U.S. waters.

Where foreign countries may be called to task for riding roughshod on their environment, there will often be a foreign corporation, an outsider to their nation, who has set the example for them, and that corporation may be from the USA.

Offshore of Africa, I saw no fish, except for one small shark that swam off at high speed upon seeing me. Only a southbound dolphin 'highway', just east of where we were anchored for weeks, gave testimony to other life forms in that great, gray-green expanse.

As with a British diver that I worked with off the coast of Africa, the first environmental concern is to stay alive. In his case, he was instructed to cut off a pipeline from its riser, near where several other pipelines and their risers were also clamped to the legs of the platform. After some discussion and drawings made by the engineer of which one of these lines were to be cut, the diver went to work. Fortunately for him, the water depth was fairly shallow, so when he was blown to the surface by the oil gushing from the pipeline, he was only well-greased, but otherwise unhurt, if a bit mortified.

The pipeline he had been told to cut was, it turned out, the wrong pipeline, one that was still full of oil and under great pressure. In another such instance, a diver was killed. Fortunately, I have not yet been 'up', that is, when your turn comes 'up', in rotation to perform this particular task. If that ever happens, I guess I will be very stubborn about verification from several sources as to whether it is a 'live' pipeline, one with gas or oil passing through it under high pressure. One method of checking this for yourself would be to get to the bare metal of the pipeline, which will be necessary for you to strike an arc to start burning with an oxy-arc torch.

Crude oil is hot, not scalding, but pretty warm. Often, it makes a sound, like stress noises, when under the pressures of passing through a pipeline. You might give the pipeline the touch-test, taking off a glove to feel if the metal is warmer than the water, and for a moment, turn off your free-flow, and listen.

Of particular concern to divers is the poison inherent to anti-fouling paint, marine coatings that deter sea growth from occurring on underwater surfaces, such as ship and boat hulls, docks, etc.

The most toxic of these paints have been outlawed by international treaties, after studies showed that these paints poisoned even the oyster beds near ship channels. These paints can kill you, or make you very sick. Although they are now outlawed it is assumed many of the ships that were coated with these toxins did not rush to drydock to have them removed.

As a contractor, I considered a contract to clean the hulls of the Navy hydrofoil squadron at Key West, Florida. A stipulation of the contract was that the divers cleaning those hulls be required to be sealed in their diving dress to protect them from the anti-fouling paint on the hull surfaces. Only a year before, I had inspected the runners and hull of the Navy hydrofoil 'Aries' where it had run aground in the shallows near Port Aransas, on the Texas coast. No mention of toxic paint was made to me then, and I made the dive in a wet suit with scuba gear. I seem to have no ill effects, but I was not cleaning and roughing the paint, which regenerates its toxins.

With that in mind, it may be that hulls coated with this killer paint say still pose a threat even after new coats of less toxic marine coatings have been applied over them, if and when the process of cleaning them might grind through the newer paint to older, previous coatings. I know of no test by which those paints may be identified.

Coral may become a memory. The reef that Pennecamp Park stands upon once stretched thousands of miles, through what is now the American midwest, northward through Wyoming and Montana to the Canadian northwest. Its legacy to those regions exists today, in the form of limestone and marble, often marked by coral and shellfish images, fossils from the Pleistocene period, a mere 125,000 years ago. It is the material for building blocks, mortar and concrete, and the marble makes for fine, sculpted statuary.

Of world-wide coral formations, a recent study indicates that one-tenth has succumbed or is succumbing to pollution in several forms, while an ever-increasing area is being picked, ripped off, and poisoned in order to decorate the living-room aquariums around the planet.

> OF WORLD-WIDE CORAL FORMATIONS, A RECENT STUDY INDICATES THAT ONE-TENTH HAS SUCCUMBED OR IS SUCCUMBING TO POLLUTION

The U.S. Government has just implemented ongoing studies to try and reverse this trend. Perhaps these reef-raiders, the very poor fishermen of coral-reef locations, could be the crux of the campaign to save the reefs. At a couple of dollars a day, they might be encouraged to make their meager pay by resurrecting, rather than destroying the coral.

The best poachers in the swamps of Louisiana, I am told, are hired away from their work by the Fish and Game Department, to become the best Fish and Game Wardens. This has not only reversed the demise of the wildlife in those swamps, but has saved many a traditional, school-trained Warden from a watery grave in some lost bayou. You sure can get lost in a Loosyana bayou. . . .

In recent times, human populations in coastal regions of the tropical Pacific — the location of 80% of the earth's coral species — has depended in large part on the fishing and other marine enterprises, the trapping of tropical fish, or taking the corals, all for export. Meanwhile, the pollution that the population density creates is taking its toll. And now comes global warming. If public awareness can boycott markets for anything from grapes to black-market ivory, the research findings on coral death issues may be the turning point, given enough publicity, worldwide. Be sure to describe these ideas with some other person, that is, pass the word.

The blind optimist and salvage diver in me (any salvage diver should be an optimist first) sees a future of rising oceans, perhaps increased rainfall due to the increased evaporation of ever-larger bodies of water covering the earth. Presto, we've got salvage work to lift Los Angeles, all cleanly washed, from the ocean depths, and a constant tropical rain begins sprouting up rain forests in our backyard. Corals begin appearing in deeper water than before, due to the increased penetration of sunlight into the depths. Snow can still be seen on the higher peaks of the Himalaya range.

But such projections are dangerous. We already know that the climate is changing, but cannot predict where that may take us, or if we, as a species, will even be invited to go along with the changes. Since we are responsible for these changes, and we were satisfied with the once-status quo, it is an understandable trend to return the climate and seasons to what they were. The prospect of encroaching oceans does not have the appeal to landlubbers as it may have to we amphibian Homo sapiens.

Then, wham, El Niño and La Niña are taken out by the asteroid that forever neutralizes our environmental concerns. The earth shrugs, we are gone the way of the dinosaurs. This is not the optimist speaking.

I do not expect to live long enough to see mankind busy in the salvage of items from the once-shorelines beneath the sea. However, I have made a joke of telling my coastal-dweller friends to attach buoys to items that they may wish to salvage later.

Optimism would dictate that whether or not we are able to reverse these both natural and human changes to our planet, still there is the prospect of many and new underwater projects in the future.

There was a time when, during my first visit to the Florida Keys, I went reef-picking with a friend of mine who lived there. She had moved there from southern California for the express purpose of being able to skindive year 'round. Truly, it was a beautiful place.

The living reefs off of Key Largo were all and more than I had expected, and I was gratified to help my friend collect barrels full of sea-biscuits, an interesting and numerous shellfish that looked to be related to the sand dollar.

But even while we were collecting these sea-biscuits, which were everywhere, I heard the death knell of the reef.

My friend began talking about how some shells and corals were becoming scarce, even rare, from over-picking, particularly helmet conch, and staghorn coral. She said that although much of the once-great stands of staghorn coral were gone, the government had made a preserve of some of the remaining staghorn, in an underwater park nearby, called Pennecamp Park. I listened.

She sold the several barrels of sea-biscuits the same afternoon, and gave me my share of the split. I had decided, based on what she told me, never to pick anything from the reef again, except for immediate consumption. Food for my stomach. We were both poor.

A few days later, I was packing to leave, and she asked me to stay on for a couple of days, saying that we would dive up some staghorn coral, that it was very valuable. I was shocked, having already heard her say that it was becoming so scarce, and so, the demise of the reef.

I had found only one helmet conch shell while we were diving the sea-biscuits, and it was empty. At the sight of it, her eyes had gone misty, and she had told me of the fate of the helmet conch and the staghorn coral. I was moved, and had resolved to take no more from the reef. Now, she's telling me she wants to dive up staghorn coral. What gives? Does being poor of necessity make one a hypocrite? No, thanks, I said.

Where was she going to find the staghorn coral, I asked, Pennecamp Park? She said no, that she knew the boundaries of the park, and would not be doing anything illegal, as the laws were then. It occurred to me that she might be doing her picking at night, but I did not ask. It was time to go.

In recent years I have revisited Key Largo and the reef. It is in bad shape, with much of the coral dying, or dead, of what is left. I am told that Pennecamp Park still has a nice stand of staghorn coral. The Park's underwater statue of Christ puts me off a bit, feeling as I do that a natural, living reef needs no statuary to detract from being a truly spiritual experience to the beholder.

It has been my good fortune to enter the cathedral-like caves of Takabanare reef, where perhaps nobody had ever been before me, and to descend the great stairs of Bolo Point, passing black lace sea fans, ten feet across. Any statue there was from a wreck, a sacrifice laid upon the altar of creation to the memory of mankind.

12.
TREASURE, ARCHEOLOGY AND ARTIFACTS

Yes, there really are pirates in this day and age. Some of them change boats frequently, and your boat may be their next. They may be smugglers, or they may be treasure divers, going after many treasures that archeologists would claim as their rightful. . . shall we say, 'artifacts'? Anyone can pose as an archeologist these days, even pirates in archeologist's clothing, are not an unknown phenomenon. Who checks archeologist credentials?

When a galleon is found at the bottom of some coral lagoon, and 15 million dollars worth of minted silver coins are salvaged from the wreck, are those coins all to be designated 'artifacts', and so reside in one museum or another? And how about the 400 gold bars salvaged from the British cruiser, sunk by a U-boat in the North Sea in WW II, which are not considered artifacts, but designated treasure, a profit to the salvors, alone.

The state, or nation in whose waters you may be seeking treasure will certainly be interested, and may well clap you in prison, if you are caught without the required permits and blessings of the government authority. With many governments, these permits will only be issued after a considerable greasing of palms. And then, you may be awarded half of what you salvage, the rest going to the sponsor politicians.

On the 'High Seas', that is to say, outside of any government's jurisdiction, it is a potential free for all, one with claim jumpers and pirates to be concerned with, where no law but the Captain's prevails. Go well armed, and keep a watch posted. Let no other vessel come close to yours without identifying themselves, an identification that you can verify. You would be well advised to be that careful within territorial waters also, even if you are merely taking a pleasure cruise. I emphasize, yes, there really are pirates in these times, maybe as many, or more, than in the past. You don't hear a lot about them because, as the saying goes, 'dead men tell no tales'.

If you still want to go in search of that treasure, consider this: the State may try to take it all away from you. I was told by a diver that he had found the missing boat, listed as such in the log of the Powell expedition, explorers of the Colorado River through the Grand Canyon in the 19th century.

figure 34- A long-tom cannon, probably British.

His description of the boat, still fairly intact in its watery grave, convinced me that he was really on to something. Unfortunately, he was unable to get the U.S. Parks Department to budge on their total claim to the boat, which lies within the boundaries of their jurisdiction, and so it remains, unfound by the diver-archeologist the Parks Dept. called in to search for it. The discovering diver, wanting some part of the claim, would give no information as to its location to the Parks Dept.

Mel Fisher, a singular success story in the realm of treasure diving, lived on beans for years until he struck his first big treasure find. The state immediately confiscated it, and there ensued a 7-year battle in the courts, with Fisher finally being awarded all he had found. When he went to claim his treasure, he found that a lot of it was missing from state vaults.

With robot technology combining outer and inner-space tracking, the collective thousands of sunken ships that litter the sea floor may be raised again to the light, some of them, like ancient time capsules, will carry messages from the past.

> **SUNKEN SHIPS, LIKE ANCIENT TIME CAPSULES, WILL CARRY MESSAGES FROM THE PAST**

One of my clients rented a robot and spent time surveying a reef some 100 miles off the Texas coast. I warned the client that a friend of mine had logged more than 700 dives on the same site, had been harried by claim jumpers, and had finally been hauled into court by environmentalists. The case dragged on for 2 years. I was told that nothing was ever found to confirm that it was in fact a wreck site. But who, knowing of what might then befall them, would ever say anything if they did find something?

Such are the murky waters of treasure diving.

I was recruited by someone I'd known from our high school days to join his treasure quest, to a lost reef in the Caribbean. Before we ever got underway, there was a plot by some of the crew members to steal the map with the famous X on it. That mutiny defused, the Captain and Mate of our vessel jumped ship in Key West. The

figure 35- Elated crew members display ivory tusks, possibly part of a slave ship's cargo, found on a reef in the Bahama Islands.

replacement Captain ran us aground on that extremely dangerous reef when we finally got to it. Intrigues, paranoia and talk of murder became the fare, like a bad Jack London novel. That I slept well may have been a contributing factor, in that I snore, or so it is alleged. I must tape a sleep session.

In this atmosphere, although we found precious artifacts that indicated the presence of treasure, I'm glad we found no solid gold. My attempt to counsel these essentially sport divers to employ a robot on their next expedition fell on deaf ears. My thought was that, since the reef top was covered by no wore than 30 feet of water, any large portions of wrecks would have been washed into deeper water by storms over the years.

They dove only into red ink on their next foray, and as often happens when you project any grand course across the seas, the weather kept them shut down. So it is that they went broke, short of their goal, but they were not broken up on the killer reef, where so many must have lost their lives, with their ships.

The greatest single treasure artifact found in the seas is a small, gold cross inset with large emeralds, found in a wreck near the Island of Bermuda, by the famous treasure diver from that island, Tom Tucker. He donated it to the island museum, and they kept it under glass and under guard for years until persons unknown switched a plastic replica for it.

Being familiar with John Steinbeck's masterpiece, *The Pearl*, and *Treasure of Sierra Madre* by B. Traven, I can only testify at this time that greed as portrayed in those stories is the major detriment to the success of any such venture. Like cocaine, it seems to envelope the participants in an evil that cancels out the best laid plans

My most valued reward from the time spent at the lost reef was to hear the late, great Peter Throckmorton, Ph.D. Marine Archeologist of note, in his discourse relating to the objects we had brought back from the reef. Being a student of history, I found his assessments of the cannon, jewelry, ivory tusks, shoe buckles, and fluted-muzzle bronze parrot gun to be fascinating and informative.

Dr. Throckmorton came aboard only after we had returned from two months on the reef, and he was necessary to giving the expedition an archeological status, along with the Marine Studies Department of an American University.

Our combined load of salvaged items indicated that a galleon, a Dutch trader, a British Man'O'War, and a slave ship had run onto the reef in the small area that we had investigated.

figure 36- *Diver using hookah gear, fanning sand for coins or other items that might be found.*

You may be interested to know that men's shoe buckles have had two periods of popularity in history, pre-dating engineer boots. And, should you find ivory tusks laying around in the Caribbean, if they have no scrimshaw or carving done to them, are probably the once-cargo of a slave ship. What tragedies may have taken place on this knob of coral, one can only imagine.

My only dive on a sunken treasure galleon came when I was instructed to place marker buoys on the location of the wreck, sunk in a pass near Coche Island, off the coast of Venezuela. The lay barge I was employed by was laying pipeline to the Island of

figure 37- Ribs of a much-worked wreck off of Sombrero Key, Florida, where divers still find an occasional sheathed rapier or a gold doubloon from time to time.

figure 38- A bombast cannon minted in Brussels, Belgium, in the 17th century. Shoe buckles and gold lockets festoon the coral encasing it. Probably a Dutch trader.

Margarita, and the Venezuelan Government did not want us to disturb the site of the galleon, which they intended to make into an underwater park.

I was surprised to find that the ribs and keel of the galleon were still much intact, and that there were piles of clumped silver coins, black with oxidation, strewn everywhere. Had I then known of the chemical process by which some of the coins could have been returned to their silver luster, I might have been distracted from my mission. There were great jewfish shadowing me, as I moved through the wreck. Given enough time for them to size me up, a little man-fish in scuba gear, they might have become dangerous.

I was told that 15 million dollars worth of silver had been salvaged from the wreck when it was found, a couple of years before.

A note on Job Hunting: Take the Archeological route. Contact the Marine Studies Dept. of Stanford University, and Texas A & M, to name a couple of many such departments in universities across the U.S. Otherwise, Treasure Salvors, Inc. of Key West, Florida, has by now established a success story unequaled in treasure finding. Good Luck.

13.
COMING UP FREE

Once you have hurriedly entered the decompression chamber, remember not to strap that oral-nasal oxygen mask on your face, but rather, hold it in place with one hand, while holding your copy of this book in the other. Avoid going to sleep during your decompression period.

figure 39- **This dogface is probably the result of too many collective years with his snoot crowded into an oral-nasal breathing mask, such as the oxygen mask that now awaits you in the decompression chamber. He may offer you a drag on that fag but take care to keep the cigarette far away from the oxygen.**

PLATE 9—IN PREPARATION FOR THE PLUNGE

PLATE 10-PILES ARE DRIVEN THROUGH LEGS INTO SEA FLOOR. LATER, THEY WILL BE FILLED WITH CONCRETE

PLATE 11—THE DECOMPRESSION CHAMBER IS MOUNTED ON A BARGE FOR EASIEST ACCESS BY DIVERS

PLATE 12—OCEAN OIL SPILLS ARE AN EXAMPLE OF ENVIRONMENTAL DIVING CONCERNS

figure 40- *The top of the derrick crane will be the last you'll see of the derrick barge. You're going home.*

Regarding transport, you may prefer a crew boat ride to that of a helicopter flight, given a choice. There are certain hazards with either mode of transportation. Occasionally, 'copters go down, and crew boats sink. Odds are, you'll never meet with either problem. Consider, just in case, which situation are you better prepared to deal with? If you have recently made a deep dive, you do not want to fly, or it might bring on the 'bends',

OCCASIONALLY, 'COPTERS GO DOWN, AND CREW BOATS SINK. ODDS ARE, YOU'LL NEVER MEET WITH EITHER PROBLEM

In tropical waters such as the summertime brings to the Gulf of Mexico, one may observe an abundance of sea creatures by day, and at night, the phosphorescence of these waters appears like a great green flame in the wake of a fast-moving crew boat.

figure 40- Which one would you designate as driver?

The bar, located not far from the dock where you come ashore may be visited by the diving crew for one beer. Strategically placed, this bar caters to all manner of sea dogs, be they corsairs or coastguard, fishermen or divers. Tradition holds that you have that beer. Tradition also dictates that you will pay for your tender's food and drink while in transit, but not gambling, drugs, or hookers such as may be encountered in the same bar. Stay with the crew, and keep a low profile. The bartender may double as the local sheriff.

14. FREE DIVING

Free diving is almost free, only requiring some sort of controlled leap into a body of water, a plunge on purpose and with purpose, and occasionally, among porpoises.

Possibly you will have a snorkel in your mouth and strapped to your head in such a way that you can lie face down in the water and look around while you breath. This is fun, and there are ways to make a living from this technique.

Imagine you are a novice, flippers propelling you through weightlessness toward the sea, like a young salmon. Moving through some calm bay or lagoon toward the blue void of the open sea . . . but wait! Before you do that you must learn to purge, clear your ears. You do this in shallow water, making 6- and 8-foot dives. Once the membrane that controls these bodily functions is strengthened by a few such dives, it will become easier to clear, until finally it happens automatically.

Flash ahead a few months, and you will find a budding damned purist who sneers at scuba divers, those group-oriented, safety-obsessed accidents waiting to happen, balling up like a bunch of sea lions and entangling themselves in a jumble of gadgetry, computers clacking against weightbelts, and the rumble and squeal of their breathing apparatus scaring off the fish.

You swim away, a mile, then two miles. It's peaceful here, lying motionless, afloat in your wet suit, gazing down at the garden below. Lunch time. You pull the plastic bottle of punch out of your net bag, which hangs on the light inner tube that you tow on a string. There are sandwiches there, too, and an old Kodak camera, all wrapped in separate ziploc bags. You have taken special pains to tape the edges of the camera's ziploc bag, and can dive it to a depth of fifteen feet.

You and your friend are spending the weekend looking for evidence of an ancient wreck, a Manila galleon, that may have foundered on this coast. You seek the telltale shards of crockery, perhaps of fine chinaware, somewhere in glaring white sand and emerald green of the sea floor below you. After lunch, you begin crisscrossing the shallow waters nearby, looking, for any sign of the wreck.

Far away, the scuba divers are rinsing off their gear, and putting it away in their storage sheds and garages, where it may remain for weeks, months, possibly years between usings. These scuba divers have not made a bond with the sea. It is a place they visit, underwater for a half hour or an hour, and put it away in time to watch the game on TV.

Wearing wide-view masks that provide peripheral vision, you have learned to avoid splashing with your fins, and so, swimming silently, you approach and mingle with schools of fish, or pounce on a lobster. The broken dish you found, half buried in the sand, is now secured in the net bag, and you are headed in, toward the surf of an incoming tide. You wonder just how powerful the surf will be, as you study the white water of wave crests ahead of you, pounding toward the beach. As you enter the surf line, you are raised high by a wave as it begins to crest, and the buoyancy of your tube and wetsuit cause you to be propelled at high speed toward the beach as the wave crashes in a thunder of white foam around you, racing toward shore. You feel and see and taste the ocean's power and glory.

Perhaps you have considered surfing, but now as you realize your addiction to free diving, it is obvious that you would only use the surfboard as a substitute for the no-cost inner tube that serves you now. Or perhaps you have become as addicted to surfing as you were once were addicted to free diving. The sea may engulf you, in many ways. I'm sure you have friends who have that 'perfect wave' fixation, who work night shift in some factory so that they may have their days on the waves. When do they sleep?

Your friends have let go of the inner tube and have been thoroughly drubbed by the wave that sped you to the shoreline. Now, laughing and cursing, they shake the sand and water out of their ears, while searching the water's edge for a missing fin.

Be warned that the power of surf can be deceiving. When entering through a surf line, test the power of the waves before you completely commit to swimming through them. I came closer to drowning in a powerful surf, so strong that it would neither let me swim out through it nor allow me to return to the beach, than in any other instance I can recall.

Before I tell you that story, I want to tell you about a free diver who booked passage from Hong Kong to Java aboard a Chinese junk. After a day at sea, the junk (an ancient style of wooden boat historically used by Chinese seafarers) sank in a storm, and the free diver found himself adrift in a stormy night in the south China sea. Still fairly intact, he had his fins, mask, snorkel, and a spear. Riding out the tempest, he dove beneath torrent wind-blown waves, and then rode high on giant swells into a new dawn. A tiny speck on a vast ocean, he felt a current carrying him toward the rising sun.

A TINY SPECK ON A VAST OCEAN, HE FELT A CURRENT CARRYING HIM TOWARD THE RISING SUN.

Scuba might have been of some use to this man because, when he had used up the air in the cylinder, it would float. As it happened, this diver chanced upon a large plank that may have floated free from the junk. Not large enough for him to climb upon, still it was broad, and afforded him shade from the sun.

In my mind at least, I was with that free diver when I found myself swept away in a strong current, headed toward the coast of Brazil which was about ten miles to my west. I had stopped yelling and waving (a whistle can come in handy) at the tugboat, moored where I had begun my scuba dive, now far away on the horizon. I had ditched the twin scuba bottles, their air expended, since I wore a wetsuit, which provided me all the flotation I would need.

Adrift! It was time to return to the instincts and adapt, swept along like a tiny plankton animal toward an unknown shore. Now, diving alone is not my preference, and it has only become standard in commercial diving in recent times that scuba divers work in pairs. But in this situation, or so I thought, it would only mean that a pair of us were swept away, instead of me, alone. I had no choice but to be there, at one with creation; mercifully, it was not the will of the Creator that I perish. The tugboat had spotted me, and, casting off its mooring lines and blowing its whistle, it headed in my direction!

It was the thought of that free diver whose junk had been wrecked in the south China sea, that came to my aid, reassured me, and made me fairly confident that I would make that shore, some ten miles distant.

What happened to that free diver in the south China sea? He was caught up one night in the nets of a Japanese trawler, and poured out on the after deck with a pile of flopping fish, his instincts urging him to return immediately to the dark sea of which he had become a part.

There was a time when, living on a rural stretch of coast, I became somewhat accustomed to free diving alone. There were no other divers to buddy-up with, and the sea was at my door, telling me to come out and play.

I would spend hours outside the surf line, and return with a bounty of abalone, kelp bass, and perhaps a yellowtail jack, or grouper. I developed the capacity to dive, holding my breath, to a 100- foot depth, although I would do so only occasionally, to investigate something briefly. My usual 'cruising range' was 40- and 50-foot dives, plunging down to return slowly to the surface, turning as I ascended, looking all around me in every direction. I was both the hunter and on the lookout for something that might be hunting me.

Thirty-odd years later, after having gone into oilfield diving and making dives in various oceans, rivers and seas, I returned to the once remote shoreline of my early free diving days to find fleets of surfers and scores of Atpacs and Buoyancy Compensators floating passenger scuba divers along at various depths, like gas balloons of the underwater.

A once-distant city had grown to millions in population, and reached up and down the coast, bringing with it the proliferation of surf and scuba shops, traffic jams and parking tickets. Worse, the marine animal life is so dissipated that serious taboos have been invoked to preserve what is left. What to do? Hunt with a camera. A good picture is worth a thousand . . . dollars. A good video, worth a lot more.

A GOOD PICTURE IS WORTH A THOUSAND .... DOLLARS. A GOOD VIDEO, WORTH A LOT MORE

In order to record some of the magnificent panoramas one can see with the naked eye, I have found it necessary to paint the scenes from memory with acrylic and oil paints, since the field of depth and light refraction make it most difficult to photograph at range. If you are a free diver, you know what is there and what you have seen. You have spent some time there.

To get into the proper spirit for your free-diving experience, I would suggest several films that deal with the subject, to be viewed in the following order. The first would be the silver-screen epic, *South of Pago-Pago*, about bad guys and pearl divers. The second would be *The Last Paradise*, a cinemascope film in color made by a French film company that includes some of the best underwater footage I have ever seen. It is a short subject, perhaps 30 minutes in duration, and you'll wish it was much longer.

The last of the films I recommend is entitled *The Big Blue*, about real people who make big bucks holding their breath for long periods of time while doing any one of a number of things underwater. This is a recent film, and contains a rivalry between free divers over who can do it deeper and longer. It is claimed that these divers have altered their metabolism to one that is comparable to that of dolphins, allowing them extended time at depth while holding their breath.

I became a clock watcher in my teens while still in school, sitting still as I watched the second hand move slowly through one, then two, then thirty seconds, and finally two and a half minutes before I took a breath. The teacher would look strangely at me, panting heavily at the end of my 'dive,' in the back of the classroom.

It has since been determined that holding your breath for a period exceeding one and a half minutes is a limit beyond which brain cells die at an accelerated rate. I have seen the effect of this in a friend who was the most fanatical spearfisherman of my (possibly damaged) memory.

He would spend so much time in the summer months plunging to depths while holding his breath that he would become 'punchy,' slurring his speech, drooping eyelids, and zero attention span. But, come late September, his faculties would have returned, being forced from his daily hours in the kelp beds by school and finally, the weather.

So, it would seem that the damage was not of a permanent nature.

A short story about spearfishing and free diving: Two friends arrived one day from the city just as I was about to go spearfishing. They accompanied me to the empty beach, and were amazed when I returned from the water, not having spent more than five minutes in the surf, with a 30-pound yellowtail impaled on my spear. They were not divers and did not know that it was the luckiest catch I had ever made, spearing one in the surf, but instead assumed that, desiring a fish, I had but to enter the sea and get one.

There is little 'sport' to spearfishing, in that if a fish has ever been hunted, you will never get close enough to spear it. On the other hand, if a fish has not been hunted, it is liable to be curious enough to swim right up to you, affording a good photograph. So it is that you may want to 'hunt' with your camera in the less trampled areas of the oceans, such as many tours to exotic locations offer. Feed the morays, the dolphins, and so forth. Scuba shops offer many of these tours, and who knows how many atolls are out there still to this day which have had virtually no divers visit them, as yet undiscovered by the thundering herd.

Free diving is the most physical type of diving. You may find yourself swimming against an outgoing tide, at the end of a day during which you have expended much of your energy while diving through kelp jungles and grottoes in the reef. It's getting late, and the cliffs that mark the shoreline are but a dark strip along the horizon toward which you swim. This is a challenge that you would do better to avoid, by consulting tide tables, available at most bait and tackle stores.

Free diving is the most relaxed type of diving. You may lie for long periods, not moving a muscle, like a glass-bottom boat with a submarine option, watching the garden below you.

That you feel comfortable and capable in the sea, and that you develop an instinctive connection with this mother of creation is important to how you may live, both of and outside the ocean, in whatever path you travel, be it scuba and the various diving mediums in underwater projects, or a space shuttle to the stars, or the many roads between. Enjoy, and live a long life while allowing other creatures to do so, but watch the tide tables, and look before you leap.

I should note two recent triumphs that underline the particular capabilities of women in the art and dance of free diving. Tanya, of Grand Cayman, the Caribbean has set a record with a free dive to 180 feet. Runner-up is Mehgan, of the Florida Keys, with a free dive to 165 feet. Imenja, the Lorilei, Mermaids all, I salute you. Many islands depend on their divers for their livelihood.

The free divers that I most admire are the Ama of Shirahama, Japan. These women are a departure from the classic, demure visage of Japanese womankind. In reading about them in the book of the above name by Anthropologist Doctorate Candidate Ms. Bethany L. Grenald, I am impressed that there are some attributes shared by divers of either sex, the world over, that do not correspond with any other group of individuals, and there is no doubt in my mind that it comes from a kinship with the sea.

Not only are these (mostly) female divers true professionals, but they have made the necessary adjustments, actually set themselves limitations in what they take from the sea to insure that the pearls, abalone, various seaweeds and marine animals will not be depleted for coming generations. They are the subjects of some ancient, beautiful Japanese art, and of modern pop culture and myth, as well.

In taking the tone that I have sometimes taken in describing scuba divers, I do not wish to diminish the importance and special uses of breathing apparatus that are more technical than the simple snorkel, but would emphasize that there may be good reason to be comfortable in the sea before going deep into it. If it ever happens that your breathing equipment, be it scuba or hardhat gear, stops feeding you air, try to distract your mind from your need for air. Practice not thinking, and swim like hell while exhaling slowly. Be with that free diver in the south China sea. He may be able to help you out of this situation, and some others.

15.

FISHISTORIES
Dedicated to Roy Connover, Morgan city

The Jonah story may have its origin in some ancient encounter with a jewfish, which is the largest of the grouper family of fishes. Where it may have gotten its name, jewfish, lends weight to the speculation of Jonah having been swallowed in the Old Testament, in one of the oldest fish stories. Who knows how large a jewfish might become, given enough groceries in terms of fish populations preceding the advent of long-line fishing boats, and seine nets? Not to mention unwary semites splashing around.

It has been pretty well established that these giants do sometimes swallow human beings in modern times. Ethnicity does not seem to enter into their menu considerations, but rather, their needed caloric intake to sustain body weights of a thousand pounds and more.

Smaller groupers have become accustomed to the presence of divers, and if they have not been hunted by spear fishermen, become friendly, even, a nuisance, if you are working against the clock.

In many instances you will be required to clean some underwater surface, perhaps a ships hull or leg of a platform, of marine animals. Barnacles, mussels, oysters, corals will be broken and smashed and added to the cloud of sea-soup around you, a feast for the little fishes. Larger fish dart in, eating the small ones and then suddenly, they all disappear, as a shadow crosses over you. You may look up from your task to see that the top predator in the food chain has arrived, and as with so many things, your mind will provide you with all of the information you may have stored regarding this potential danger. For jewfish that I perceived to be large enough to swallow me, I would remember that they swallow in a way similar to a slurp gun, sucking in the morsel, as if inhaling it. Gulp. So, connect with something they can't swallow, something you can cling to, maybe the oilfield platform that you are working on, or one of the massive ribs of a sunken treasure ship. Call for help. Tell the standby diver to hang some large hooks on his harness, and come help you catch this fish.

Any fish will usually size you up for awhile before coming close to you. During that time, you are sizing up the fish. If it is big enough to worry about, don't turn your back on it, and tell them topside to pick you up, before the fish may start getting close enough to do

figure 43- The author with moray meal, 1959.

you possible harm. Following this plan, a diver, working in the North Sea, was being pulled into the diving bell, when the sea bass (jewfish) swallowed him up to his armpits. The other diver in the bell reached down, with a screwdriver, and poked the fish in the eye. The fish let go, but spent the next 24 hours hanging around the job site, apparently waiting for the next diver.

A diver from Morgan City, LA was working off Trinidad in the early 1970's, and may have been swallowed by a jewfish. They picked up his gear, and he was not in it. Near the oilfield platform that he had been working on was a large coral reef around which a number of big jewfish were to be seen, and it was thought that perhaps one of these had swallowed him. Nobody could say, for sure.

Only once, in many years of diving, have I been approached directly by a shark. I was snorkeling, spear gun in hand, having just entered the water from a boat in Chimu-wan Bay, near Okinawa. I had a diving 'buddy' who had almost immediately speared a fish, and dove down and out of sight in pursuit of it. At that moment I saw three parrot fish being chased across the reef by a shark, the shark saw me, and turned to head in my direction. A gunmetal gray, short but broad, built like a 500-lb. bomb with a stubby, pointed snout, It looked nothing like the reef sharks I was accustomed to. It had slowed to a glide, checking me out, but coming head-on. All the information I had on sharks came to mind. Time stopped.

THE SHARK SAW ME, AND TURNED TO HEAD IN MY DIRECTION

The boat was only 20 feet behind me. I did not want to turn my back on this shark, but I lifted my face out of the water and hollered that a shark was approaching me. Then I dove down to the top of the reef, the counsels of Costeau, of Haas guiding me. A shark's prey is often on the surface. The shark was twenty feet from me, and closing. Spear gun in one hand, I unsheathed my knife, my backup. Prone on the coral, I prepared to shoot. For the mouth. I could now see rows of snaggly teeth, coming on. Shoot, when he was at one spears length. Shoot!...Oh, the safety was on! Flick off the safety, just in time, almost. touching the spearhead....

With a glorious, great 'whump' sound, two divers plunged into the water behind me, bursting onto the scene in a great cloud of bubbles, and the shark was gone, in a flicker. Almost as fast, I was aboard the boat, making explanations to my buddies in the water. I told them that the shark could have the ocean, I'd stay out of it. I was that frightened. They had not seen this shark. This was a shark that you did not want to see. They kept after me, 'Come on, let's hunt that shark down, get it before it gets somebody,' they coaxed me, from that scary ocean I'd just emerged from. I went back in the water, albeit with some reservations. I was glad that we did not encounter the shark. I later ID'd the shark as one of the oceans bad actors, the zambesi, or bull shark, given the latter name for their bulky shape, and the former name for their penchant for eating up people in the Zambesi River and all along the coast of South Africa. And, that's no bull.

WITH A GLORIOUS, GREAT 'WHUMP' SOUND, TWO DIVERS PLUNGED INTO THE WATER BEHIND ME, BURSTING ONTO THE SCENE IN A GREAT CLOUD OF BUBBLES, AND THE SHARK WAS GONE

I was fortunate to have seen this shark when it saw me, otherwise I would have been a sitting duck. As mentioned earlier, most potentially dangerous fish will look you over, and this one was doing just that, but without the niceties of circling me. But, I was on the surface of the water, and was not making noise such as the bubble exhalations or use of underwater tools make, and which probably scare many fish away. Often, while being 'in the work', I am so absorbed in the task at hand that I would be easy prey. Once, some unknown fish bit my communication cable in two, giving me such a yank in the process that I thought a boat's propeller had snagged my hose. Up on deck, nobody knew anything about the yank on my air hose or why I lost communication, until I found the break in the comm' wire. A really tough wire, comm' wire has a mesh of very strong stainless steel wire built into it. Something had snapped it without touching the diving hose, which it is taped to, only a few feet above where it connected to my helmet.

Young and foolish, I once killed a white-tip reef shark with an arbalete spear gun, this time with me as the aggressor. When I got the six-foot shark ashore, after worrying about the blood trail as I swam it through the surf, I realized that the spear had barely penetrated the tough skin. By fool's luck, the shaft had penetrated a little more than an inch at the only vital point possible, where the skull connects to the spine, for such a shallow puncture. I had been aiming for the shark's eye. I swore never again to initiate hostilities with another underwater predator, unless, of course, it would taste good.

Doing in-water decompression stops in the Gulf of Mexico was often a visit with very large barracudas, a curious fish that sometimes seemed to view the presence of divers as a novel entertainment. Often the 'cudas could be seen in pairs, touring the underwater worksite, stopping to peer at the diver's ladder, and the hang-

figure 44- Always remember that you are very small.

off bar, where the divers make their decompression water stops. At night, the blaze of lights from the barge would attract schools of small fish, making the hunting easier for the 'cudas.

Personally, I always thought of these fierce-looking fish as being inquisitive and rather civil, where humans were concerned, and have not heard of them attacking anyone in the Gulf. However, I know that they are much feared in the Caribbean, perhaps with good reason. Knowing they would be around, I always took pains not to wear anything that resembled a small, shiny fish. They are so fast in movement when they want to be, there would be no defense against one, if it wanted to bite you.

Barracudas were all around me one night, as I sat on the hang-off bar. One, with a large gash in its back, a wound made by a glancing blow from a spear thrown by a deckhand earlier in the day, was closest to me. It kept getting closer to me, slowly doing a sideways shuffle, one big goggle eye staring at me while its jaws opened and closed, in a display of long, sharp teeth. 'Cudas do this in order to breath, when not swimming. But I was trying out my mental telepathy to a fish-brain, trying to explain that I would never have done harm to such a nice, big 'cuda. Finally when it was almost within arms reach, I could not stand the suspense any longer. I pulled some slack on my hose, made a loop of it, and swung it at the barracuda. It disappeared like a flash of quicksilver into the darkness.

Triggerfish are the most aggressive fish that have attacked me and other divers, going for fingertips, preferably in black-dot gloves, and any other exposed flesh, maybe an earlobe, if you're diving in a mask without a hood. Fortunately, triggerfish don't get any larger than a small frying pan. But don't eat one, because they eat coral, and are poisonous. Triggers will sneak around the leg of a platform as you are putting a riser clamp on it, and grab one of your fingertips in their parrot-like beak. Ouch.

Fishistories would require at least one Giant Catfish story, so here goes: I was told that the locks on the Sabine River were jammed by a catfish SO large that divers set explosive charges on it to dislodge it. Got any comparable catfish stories?

1

16.
GOLF BALLS AND THE MIDNIGHT FROGMEN

A golf course by night is a rather surrealistic land, illuminated by a full moon, its fairways, greens, and rough areas reflecting different shades of blue-gray, contrasting with the almost white of the sand trap and inky blackness of the ponds.

Surrounded by a city, perhaps the low hum of distant traffic is to be heard, and off in the distance, a few outside lights mark the location of the golf pro's office where the electric carts sleep, getting their recharge for the morning events.

Making our approach to the closest pond from the place we parked the car, we are a little apprehensive. This is new to us, and a bit spooky. We are sensitive to the sounds of a regulator bouncing against a scuba cylinder, grabbing it quickly to quell the sound of escaping air. As we approach a stand of cattails by the water, the chirping and gurgling sounds made by its inhabitants ceases. In the distance, a dog barks.

Is that a watchman's dog, and aren't the barks getting closer? It would be better to get into the water, and submerge, rather than attempt a race to the car, which is parked at some distance from us now. Passing the stand of cattails, we quickly step into the black water, feeling the chill of it as our booties sink into the mud, and we hurriedly don our wetsuit hoods and our scuba masks.

Far off, we hear the sound of a man's voice calling, and the dog's barking ceases. Giving my regulator a test huff and puff, I resolutely clamp my teeth down on the mouthpiece and submerge, noticing that the water has a bad, rather sulfurous smell.

It was wintertime, the off-season for oilfield diving during which time someone who depends on that for their livelihood can find themselves seeking other employments, preferably of an aquatic nature. But this?

At first I scoffed at the idea of such work, diving into these fetid ponds, dense with algae and the domain of water moccasins and snapping turtles. A friend had called and suggested that we attend a recruitment meeting and seminar to be given by someone called the 'Golf Ball King.' We got there late, and ended up having lunch with the 'King,' and so had our chance on sounding him out on this golf ball thing called money.

A golf ball sized lump forms in my throat as I recall his words of wisdom, which were as follows: Always dive at night. Never chance being hit by a golf ball. Safety first. Get rich. There are thousands of balls awaiting us in the ponds of the city's many golf courses.

Night time on the golf course? Was this not trespassing? Stealing balls? No. He had contacted the courses, and there was only one which would not allow his services. And probably we could 'get in on' that course, as well, as he put it. He went on to say that he sold most of the balls back to those same courses, by his agreement with them.

He also sold rubber dry suits, manufactured by an Italian tire company, to any interested parties. Visions of Flotilla Eight, Italian frogmen, came to mind. The midnight frogmen in a frog pond. Mama mia. Golf balls.

We send him the balls, and he sends us a check. But, I did not like his price per ball, and I said I'd think it all over. That night, I made my first golf ball survey dive, under a blazing full moon.

There were some golf balls in the pond, but not many. There was some sort of critter, a muskrat, maybe, that began buzzing me in the dark water. I felt the wash go by me a couple of times before I turned on my lamp. In the murky water, I spotted what appeared to be an accelerated furball that swooshed by, just on the edge of the light, a couple of times before I could get the hell out of that pond.

As we trudged toward the car, dripping, and scraping the mud from our booties, I was considering what I had learned. I decided that I would not dive golf ponds at night. After all, golfers are trying not to hit the water, and I would stay submerged for as long as possible while diving in the ponds, during daylight. But I would first secure permission to dive the ponds, from the respective golf pros.

Soon, I had seven golf courses contracted, but only verbal contracts, and I would make my rounds to each of them about once every three months.

The golf pros that were most often in charge of all golf ball negotiations seemed to think that all of their ponds were deep, some of them, very deep.

On several occasions, hearing of some particularly deep, mysterious and perhaps bottomless pond, I thought that perhaps hard-hat gear and decompression schedules might be in order. Might this not be a pond similar to one described in a Dr. Seuss book, reaching all the way to China? A saturation diving system might be in order.

I would investigate, donning a double-cylinder scuba rig, and plunging into the subject pond. At least, I had heard no giant catfish stories, although I did sometimes see a 'harmless' water snake, of which there were three varieties. Harmless, I say, in that they were not venomous. They were well known to bite, however.

After the initial midnight frogman experience, I had opted for using my dry suit. This water, although I avoided those courses that used reclaimed sewage water, was still no joy to enter or to smell.

Literally feeling my way into the realm of the submerged golf ball business, my major ball-locator technology breakthrough came by way of my hesitance to feel around in the muck with my fingers. I found that two pieces of small-gauge pvc pipe, about the length of batons, would make a clicking sound when they came in contact with an unseen golf ball. And I could stab one of the pipes into the mud, giving me a local reference to the immediate area I was searching.

Added to the pvc pipe discovery, I learned that a large, woven plastic bag, such as is often used to contain rice, made a perfect pouch which, wrapped through my weight belt, was both handy and easily dropped with the weight belt, should it become necessary. These bags have the double advantage of not holding the water, and to some degree cleaning the golf balls, while you work.

Once the bottom of a pond gets stirred up with my groping in the mud, visibility is nil. Unless you want to take time to come to the surface, you cannot read your air pressure gauge. On several dives I had to ditch my weight and bail out, when I ran out of air. It is recommended that the diver bring a second weight belt, allowing him to retrieve the dropped weight belt in such an emergency. As to 'buddy' diving, it's okay, if you want to split the proceeds with a partner. To my knowledge, even the midnight frogmen are usually loners.

ONCE THE BOTTOM OF A POND GETS STIRRED UP WITH MY GROPING IN THE MUD, VISIBILITY IS NIL

I would sometimes encounter these frogmen, hovering near the perimeter of a course in the late afternoon as I was departing from it, with perhaps 10 or 15 five-gallon buckets full of balls riding in the back of my pickup truck. I knew that they would be wasting their time, searching ponds and sometimes lakes for the balls I had already taken.

By the same token, I would find my client's ponds empty sometimes, the work of the midnight frogmen. The golf pros would then rant and rave, swearing to enlist guard dogs and trip-flares and the like. Midnight frogmen might have to crawl under barbed-wire entanglements and avoid satellite surveillance, on some futuristic golf course.

As winter gave way to spring, and I was more and more called upon to spend days and weeks in offshore oilfield diving projects, the time lapse on my golf-course rounds increased. This is good, in that the longer time period between pond dives gave those ponds time to accumulate more errant golf balls.

Sometimes I would enter a pond to find that over the months since I had last entered it, the bottom had been filled with balls several layers deep.

Once, taking a breather at the edge of a pond, lying like a beached porpoise in the sun, and taking my chances at being whacked by a golf ball, I watched a party of four golfers play through. Two of them put a ball each in the water. While they cursed, I thought that I was definitely in the right business, bringing these lost balls back to the light of day, a catcher-in-the-rye-pond. Some of the balls had the smiling, happy-face indelibly printed on them.

WHILE THEY CURSED, I THOUGHT THAT I WAS DEFINITELY IN THE RIGHT BUSINESS

As a child I had the privilege of knowing an Irish Setter, my uncle's dog, that made a habit of intercepting golfers' balls on the nearby country club golf course. Having slammed a great drive down a lush, green fairway, the astonished golfer would see this flaming red dog emerge from the cover of a ravine, a streak of fire on a converging course with his still-bouncing golf ball. Grabbing the ball in its maw, Terra would then skulk back to the ravine, and disappear, only to turn up at my uncle's place with yet another nice golf ball. My uncle was himself a golfer, and being suspected of having put the dog up to using its genetic urge as a retriever for his own nefarious schemes, he reluctantly had to tie the dog, and otherwise contain it, to avoid having it shot by the irate ball owners.

I have seen the lust for 'Titleist,' 'Ping,' and other desirable brands of golf balls shining in the eyes of golfers loitering around my truck, eyeing the five-gallon buckets of algae-encrusted balls as I approached with yet another rice sack bulging with the objects of their obsession.

I would not, of course (no pun intended) deal balls to these golf junkies, owing to my agreements with the golf pro, and the probability that I was being observed through binoculars from the office. This golf pond diving has its own particular list of hazards.

One country club that had carved a new golf course out of a wild area of virtual mesquite jungle, and which had just recently opened, had too many snakes, and many of them of the poisonous varieties. I heard stories of snakes dropping from the limbs of trees onto passing golf carts. I knew a golfer that was bitten by a rattler on another course and decided the hazards of this new course outweighed the potential benefits. The midnight frogmen could have it all, and good luck.

Making my initial dive into one of a succession of ponds that were considered to be very deep ones, I soon found out that there was so little depth to the ponds that I could stand, water only up to my thighs, in the deepest center of these in fact shallow ponds.

I wrestled with this knowledge, knowing what the golf pro did not, that any wader could effectively salvage all three ponds, without any diving services required. But, on the other hand, part of submerging myself in these ponds was to avoid being whacked by a golf ball, was it not?

With that rationale, I continued diving these ponds with scuba, although I'm sure that my back was often exposed to, shall we say, the danger of incoming golf balls. Luckily, I never suffered a hit. Then, on my last trip to this particular golf course, it happened to be on a Sunday, the course was closed for business, and only the groundsmen were there, tidying up the greens.

I saw one of these groundsmen wading, a large rake in hand, out into the center of one of the ponds. At about the same time, several of the courses that I had agreements with decided to offset their considerable water bills by using the local treated sewage in their ponds.

The golf pro at one of these courses told me there was no potential hazard in either the chemicals used in the treatment of this 'effluent water,' or any threat of bacteria, since the chemicals destroyed all bacteria. He said the wastewater people had told him the water would even be safe to drink. Since I would of necessity be drinking at least small amounts by scuba diving in it, I decided to double-check this information.

The people at the sewage treatment plant warned that there was no guarantee that some dangerous bacteria might not get through, and do real harm. At about this same time, another cloud appeared on the 18th green, so to speak, in the form of a low-rater.

This guy appeared out of Florida, that land of golf courses, like a

Ghengis Kahn golf ball scourge, pricing so far under the competition that one after another, the Gulf coast golf divers fell before his onslaught.

Not only did he price low, but he sidelined with striping the damaged balls to be used as range balls. He compensated for his smaller return on resale of good balls by camping out, rather than suffer motel costs, and no doubt profited by volume, for it was said that he had contracted a great number of golf courses.

In more recent times, I have contacted inland diving companies at one time or another, just in my curiosity as to what line of commercial diving they were involved with, to learn that they were totally devoted to golf ball diving. And you can be sure, lurking around the perimeters of these contracted services, are the midnight frogmen, awaiting sundown.

PLATE 13–A DIVER'S WORLD IS FULL OF SIGHTS OF UNEXPECTED BEAUTY

Photo by Terry Stern

PLATE 14—DIVER HAULING PHOTO-GRAPHIC EQUIPMENT

Photo by Terry Stern

PLATE 15—UNDERWATER SCENERY OFFERS AMAZING PANORAMAS FOR ENVIRONMENTAL EXPLORATION

Photo by Terry Stern

PLATE 16-A DIVER AT WORK

Photo by Terry Stern

17.

JOB HUNTING DURING THE BLACK GOLD RUSH

Dedicated to David May

In 1969 I was working on a diving job so dangerous as to compel me to find another job before this one might kill me. Commuting daily to a port near Morgan City, LA I had been inspecting an underwater pipeline. To do this required a boat to follow me along the pipeline, while a tender handled my hose from the boat's bow, making sure that the boat did not run over me and snag my hose and chop me up with its propellers. It required an alert boat Captain to control the speed and direction of the boat. In that, this Captain was totally lacking in skills.

In Morgan City of that time, there was an oil boom in progress. Money flowed like rum through the bars along U.S. Highway 90, and jobs were got, or sold, or bought to the jukebox strains of Merle Haggard or Jefferson Airplane in psychedelic taverns and country bars.

Oilfield contractors, boat captains, drillers, mates and deckhands, roustabouts, divers and riggers, besotted and boisterous oilfield 'sailors' all, peopled these barrooms, which were open around the clock. Generally, women were in a minority, a status they seemed to relish for the attention and pursuit of them it created.

I had to remember that this was job-hunting I was doing, nursing a bourbon and scanning the faces in Lil's Elbow Room for a familiar face. Another long day would start at dawn, slogging through the mud along the submerged pipeline in black water, the whirring sound of the boats propellers close behind me.

Healthy fear would prod my career in this instance, and in the future. Guardian angels are known to take a day off, so you don't want to overwork them. Mine had been getting too much overtime.

It was rumored that Jacques Yves Cousteau was in town, shopping for American divers experienced in this first of its kind, an underwater oilfield. The submerged oilfield was expanding in a maze of wellheads arid pipelines, across the bottom of the Gulf of Mexico. It was going deeper, to the edge of the continental shelf, and not only the French, but the whole world wanted to buy into this technology.

Since I was spending my daylight hours underwater in a race with the boat that seemed intent on running me over, I had no chance to seek employment through 'normal' channels. I had been through that a year and more before, right out of diving school and with a background in military diving. Dressed in. a sport coat and tie, my resumé in hand, I had made the rounds of the oilfield diving companies in Morgan City, the fount of offshore oilfield work.

Grizzled old men peered at me, a dude from the west, like I was grist for the mill. Taking his feet off the desk and putting his gun down, (he'd been shooting tin cans through the open back door) one of these hired me. I tended divers for 8 months, pulled weeds in the company lot, painted machinery, then they started diving me. They would not fire the inept boat captain. Maybe he was related to one of my bosses. So, back to job hunting. Onward, to the next Morgan City bar, trying to remember some words in French.

Pushing through the swinging doors of the Dream State Bar, I noticed Jake 'Snake' Marvelette gesturing with his beer bottle at the man sitting next to him at the bar. Jake was a large man, his hand encompassing most of the bottle, as he jabbed the air with it, under this opponent's nose, saying, "If you don't back off, Red, I'm gonna' bust you one."

Fair enough warning, I thought, as I headed toward the far end of the bar. There was the sound of Otis Redding's blues from the jukebox, but otherwise, the room had grown quiet. I selected a stool, and signaled the bartender, a tall, thin, guy in a Beatle wig. But his eyes, like mine, were trained on Jake's confrontation down the bar.

"They call you Snake? Why, you're a . . . ," began Red, slurring a bit through his snarl.

Whap, sounded Jake's knuckles as they collided with Red's jaw. Jake had dropped his beer, hit the man, and caught the beer before it hit the floor. Red toppled like a great tree from his stool, landing hard. Men seated on either side of the combatants shoved money down the bar, and Jake amassed it in a pile in front of him, and ordered drinks for the house. Three volunteers carried Red to a booth, staggering under his bulk, and set his new drink on the table where he'd see it, when he awoke.

Adjusting to the dim light, I saw in the reflection of a mirror the couple seated in a dark booth behind me. She was the wife of a friend of mine. He was in Tampico, Mexico, on a Pemex job. Who was this guy? I wondered. Her eyes met mine in the mirror. Shiftily shifting my gaze, I felt uncomfortable.

I noticed another face peering at me from the mirror, but from under a pinball machine? A familiar face to which I turned, ignoring the couple.

"What are you doing under there, Steve?" I asked.

"Jake told me to stay here until he leaves," came the sheepish reply. I turned back to my newly arrived drink, trying to stifle a laugh. I knew the story of how Steve, an inexperienced diver-tender, had mistakenly pressured Jake in a decompression chamber to the equivalent of 300 feet depth. Despite Jake's wrathful appeals, Steve had left him at that pressure for more than an hour. Jake, succumbing to nitrogen narcosis, raptures of the deep, could do little more than giggle, and bang fee-

JAKE, SUCCUMBING TO NITROGEN NARCOSIS, RAPTURES OF THE DEEP, COULD DO LITTLE MORE THAN GIGGLE

bly on the inside of the chamber, especially since Steve had turned off the radio while he feverishly consulted his Navy Diving Manual.

Finally, realizing his mistake, Steve had called one of the divers to assist him. There followed a period of some hours before Jake was brought safely to surface pressure, and could come out of the chamber, where he had to be restrained from doing Steve great bodily harm.

Now, they had met again. Steve would stay under the pinball machine until he had finished a quart of whiskey in order to simulate raptures of the deep, and Jake departed from the bar, spake Jake, in Solomon-like wisdom. Let the punishment fit the crime.

Three men had entered the bar, their brightly-colored company jackets, blue and gold with a red diving helmet emblazoned on the back, identified them as Zargon Diving company people. I recognized one of them as the operations manager, and I was back to my job hunting concerns. I watched the three as they made polite greetings to those at the bar, wending their way past Red's large, booted feet, where they protruded from the booth.

They took the only three empty stools at the bar, on my right. On my left was someone with his head on the bar, sleeping, while a heavy-set woman embraced him, crooning, while she went through his pockets. The 'Who' could see for miles and miles and miles reverberated electronically from the jukebox.

I waited for their eyes to adjust to the gloom before speaking, was gratified when the Ops. Mgr. – I had forgotten his name – leaned forward, and hailed me.

"Hey, Zip, where you been?" came the loud query. "I've been trying to get a line on you for days," he continued.

"I moved to New Orleans, but I'm working, walking the shallow end of that pipeline that goes out to the Gulf." I replied. I had lived in Morgan City for that first year after I arrived from diving school, through my work transition from tender to diver.

"Bad job you're on," he replied, "Killed O.D. Kepp, y'know." Suspicions confirmed, I thought. I knew that Kepp had been killed while 'live-boating', such as I was doing. Someone, maybe Kepp's wife, had stenciled 'O.D. Kepp' on the outside of Lil's Elbow Room bar, a eulogy to a diver.

"You are right," I said, "And what do you have going on that I might apply to?"

"Deep water, maybe two years work," came the welcome reply. I had moved off the stool, and stepped over to where he had turned to face me. I was introduced to his companions, one of whom said, "Welcome aboard." I was transported, elated as if a death sentence had been lifted from me.

"I'll have to give Don Jarret, Inc. notice tomorrow," I said. "At least 24 hours, so he can hire somebody else to take my place." That settled, I bought them a round of drinks, we shook hands, and I headed for the door.

Passing Red in his booth, I noticed he was sitting upright, a drink in his hand, glaring at Jake's back at the bar, as I virtually hopped out the door to the strains of 'White Rabbit'.

I could not forsee that my new job would have me working in the deep blue waters of the Gulf for the two following years, doing subsea tie-ins, jet sled dredging of pipelines, riser construction and learning a variety of tasks. It was gratifying to work with and learn from some of the best free-lance divers in the industry, the same divers that I would see and work with time and again for the various diving companies in future years.

Most often, there will be a more normal process of applying for work with a given contractor. Submit your resumé by mail to the operations manager, along with a cover letter in which you should be brief and enthusiastic. An important asset to your resumé would be any letters of reference from educators and employers, that you may include. If you are applying to a small contractor, a list of your own personal diving equipment and tools of the trade would be good to include with the above items. Then call them, when you believe they have seen your resumé.

18. DIVING SCHOOLS

Technical and basic training for a career in the field of commercial diving through an accredited school is almost a must for making 'The Leap', a long step which you may view in future years as a most significant direction in your life. Preparatory to your selection of a school, you should take a long look at what it provides for your needs.

The schools that I refer to and as are listed alphabetically on the following pages are all located near or on the three coasts of the lower forty-eight states of the U.S.A.

I say 'almost a must' with the exceptions of those of you who have documented training in the Armed Services, all of which maintain some sort of diving department or division, be they commandoes in blackface or bridge builders in hard-hat gear. Be advised that where there may not be a lot of work for people versed in night landings from rubber boats, still you have had your basics in physiology, gas laws and decompression, and so might apply on the strength of that alone. However, I would recommend that you attend a school that will verse you in the application of salvage techniques, and the nuts and bolts of oilfield construction, underwater burning and welding, rigging, carpentry, and I emphasize, rigging. In the almost zero-gravity you'll often work in, how you connect rope and wire cables to objects that you want to move or set in place makes a very large difference.

There may be somewhere an inland commercial diving school, being that river work has its special conditions, and there are many inland diving contractors in places like Utah and Kansas, to name a couple, who know the waters along their shorelines, comprising thousands of miles.

Various city colleges have study programs in the Marine Sciences, at least a couple of these also offer commercial diving courses, notably Santa Barbara, California City College, and Houston, Texas.

For the aspiring diver with prison time to serve, there is Chino State Prison diving school in Southern California, which produces some Hands, often with many years of training, and the ability to shrug off long periods of isolation in distant oceans.

The civilian school that I attended stressed safety, and among other things, we were told to never attempt to cut concrete with oxy-arc burning gear. A friend who had attended another school was killed when be tried doing just that. Concrete explodes when you gouge it with a burning electrode. Perhaps his school had not included that information in his training, an example of the diversity of instruction to be had out there, in which the details may make a very big difference.

Your diving school instructor is the key. It was my good fortune to have as my instructor a Mr. Morris Talbot, a man gifted for his ability to breath life into the text of the U.S. Navy Diving Manual, which is THE single and only center of the core of your diving studies. You may obtain a copy of this vital reference book through the U.S. Printing Office. I would suggest that you take up reading it and understanding its messages, once you have finished this book.

THE U.S. NAVY DIVING MANUAL IS THE SINGLE AND ONLY CENTER OF THE CORE OF YOUR DIVING STUDIES

As with any trade or professional school, a major benefit of attending is that of the friends and contacts you will make there, people who are going into the business and with whom you will share a camaraderie, possibly for the rest of your life. After all, this is a new life you are stepping into.

One of the major diving companies that is involved in worldwide oilfield diving work established their own in-house diving school, and made a practice of offering the top 10% of each graduating class a one-year contract to work for the parent diving company at comparatively low wages. This set-salary amount would not vary, regardless of how much overtime the graduate might work, and no depth pay was included, regardless of how deep they might be required to dive.

This would apply only in work outside the continental limits of the U.S.A., so that Federal Labor Law might not be as easily invoked.

The graduate would begin their contract as a tender, which is normal procedure with all companies. During that year, the graduate might or might not set foot on shore beyond, say, his arrival on board a barge in the Straits of Malacca, and his departure from it a year later, at the company's convenience. Or, the graduate might find himself working at a depth of 400 feet in the North Sea, alongside divers of Chinese, British, South American and all the foreign nations, some of whom speak fairly good English, and whose pay scales are even less than the graduate's. Divers from third-world countries usually do not have any recourse in a court of law if injured or killed in some faraway ocean, as do American divers. So it is that much of the foreign work has gone to other than American divers, even though the parent company may be a U.S. Corporation that has bought out a foreign company.

A great post graduate education with pay, you say? Yes, I have worked alongside many of these 'graduates', and recognized that they had been through a deeper grist-mill, than my own experience with the inept crew-boat skipper.

They had learned through surviving their experience. When they were able to look around in the industry and discover higher pay scales they might apply to, they changed companies. Some of these graduates took it a step further, and partnered themselves in their own company, one that paid the divers a good wage scale by diverting some more of their profits to pay for divers of good, established reputations, in effect, experience.

I will not speculate on the number of casualties incurred by using these graduates of little experience in combination with foreign divers of possibly less experience, but I will admit to hearing firsthand accounts of some tragedies from these contract-graduates, and at least one such account from the brother of a foreign diver, whose family could not learn any details of his brother's death in the harbor of Rio de Janiero.

One thing is certain, to advertise diving services as being Deeper Cheaper is a corporate sales ploy that is hard to beat. But rather than be used in this manner, I would suggest that the graduate student make a serious survey of prospective diving employers through the current numerous sources of information, be they trade journals, web sites, or municipal power companies to name just a few.

For those of you with no previous experience in the underwater realm, I would strongly suggest that you enroll in a scuba training class at one of your local scuba dive shops, so as to get the initial feel of what it is like to breath while underwater and deal with the feeling of weightlessness, and to have your first instruction in the vital areas of safety underwater. By so doing, you may be better able to determine whether commercial diving is in fact what you want to do.

The school I attended in 1967 was then the only V.A. accredited school, so I did not have a selection to choose from. Our training took place in a classroom, also in a large vat of black water set in a cavernous tin building adjacent to the classroom, and in the polluted estuary canal behind the building. Once you left the surface, you were in total darkness. Our only diving dress was 'Heavy Gear', meaning Mark V copper helmets with breastplates and lead shoes. The leaky suits were of canvas-covered rubber.

This gear was developed in the 1880's, and like little diving bells, the Mark V gear is still a very viable diving medium where the water is rough, cold and dark.

My only distinct memory of the sessions in the vat is that of the classmate I was assigned to help dress-out preceding his daily dive. He would mostly be very hung-over, and I would close his faceplate as soon as possible to cut off the smell of his breath. He did not like that, the faceplate being closed before it was absolutely necessary, and would begin fussing at me. I would then turn, off the dive radio, until he got in the tank. Then, he'd go to sleep as often as not. A party-imperative animal. Later heard be had a job retrieving torpedoes. Another went to salvage the iron of Scapa Flo, another to salvage the Andrea Doria, a major cruise ship.

My choice was then the oilfield, along the Gulf Coast, where I'd never been. As it turned out, it was a good choice, a mixed blessing. I lost some good friends to the grist mill. Be careful.

Given those questions and directions in these times, I would be more inclined to go into the new, high-tech possibility of deep-water salvage, in places where the wrecks of antiquity might be layered.

There exists a National Association of Commercial Divers that maintains a clearing house for information on education, schools, and underwater technology in its many facets. You can get them on the web at NUP.//NAOCU.ORG/ or write to them at P.O. Box 915, Charlottesville, VA 22902-0915 and get the real scoop. FAX them at (603) 415-3532 or phone them at (804) 286-8837. Otherwise, you may choose to contact any of the private and public scbools listed below.

272 South Fries Avenue, Wilmington, CA 90744
(310) 834-2501, (800) 432-3483, Fax (310) 834-7132

2500 South Broadway, Camden, NJ 08104
(609) 966-1871, (800) 238-3483, Fax (609) 541-4355

4315 11th Avenue, NW, P.O. Box 70667, Seattle, WA 98107-0667
(206) 783-5542, (800) 634-8377, Fax (206) 783-2658

Marine Technology Program
721 Cliff Drive, Santa Barbara, CA 93109
(805) 965-0581, ext. 2426/2427, Fax (805) 963-7222

10840 Rockley Road, P.O. Box 721738, Houston, TX 77272-1738
(713) 530-0202, (800) 321-0298, Fax (713) 530-9143

For more information contact:
Association of Commercial Diving Educators
John Schwitters (310) 834-2501

ABOUT THE AUTHOR

Tony Smith trained for scuba diving in the Marine Corps, after which he took courses in Business Administration and Creative Writing at UC Berkeley. He graduated in Commercial Diving from the Coastal School of Diving in Oakland, CA, in 1967, and since then has pursued a career in diving that has taken him to the depths off three continents. He presently travels between Arizona and Mexico, and is making a photographic study of the Sea of Cortez.